P9-BJM-482

CONTROVERSY!

Alternative Energy Sources

Kathiann M. Kowalski

Marshall Cavendish
Benchmark
New York

This book is dedicated to my husband, Michael George Meissner.

ACKNOWLEDGMENTS

The author gratefully thanks the following people for sharing their insights and comments: Mark Bello, National Institute of Standards and Technology; Jennifer Lash, Living Oceans Society; Maria Maack, Icelandic New Energy; Ma Amin, Embassy of China; Jim Owen, Edison Electric Institute; Angelika Pullen, Global Wind Energy Council; Tony Rothman, Princeton University; Carla Shoemaker, Ph.D., Agronomy and Soils, Auburn University.

Copyright © 2011 Marshall Cavendish Corporation
Published by Marshall Cavendish Benchmark
An imprint of Marshall Cavendish Corporation

All rights reserved.

No part of this publication may be reproduced, stored in a retrieval system or transmitted, in any form or by any means, electronic, mechanical, photocopying, recording, or otherwise, without the prior permission of the copyright owner. Request for permission should be addressed to the Publisher, Marshall Cavendish Corporation, 99 White Plains Road, Tarrytown, NY 10591.
Tel: (914) 332-8888, fax: (914) 332-1888.
Website: www.marshallcavendish.us

This publication represents the opinions and views of the author based on Kathiann M. Kowalski's personal experience, knowledge, and research. The information in this book serves as a general guide only. The author and publisher have used their best efforts in preparing this book and disclaim liability rising directly and indirectly from the use and application of this book.

Other Marshall Cavendish Offices:
Marshall Cavendish International (Asia) Private Limited, 1 New Industrial Road, Singapore 536196 • Marshall Cavendish International (Thailand) Co Ltd. 253 Asoke, 12th Flr, Sukhumvit 21 Road, Klongtoey Nua, Wattana, Bangkok 10110, Thailand • Marshall Cavendish (Malaysia) Sdn Bhd, Times Subang, Lot 46, Subang Hi-Tech Industrial Park, Batu Tiga, 40000 Shah Alam, Selangor Darul Ehsan, Malaysia

Marshall Cavendish is a trademark of Times Publishing Limited.

All websites were available and accurate when this book was sent to press.

Library of Congress Cataloging-in-Publication Data
Kowalski, Kathiann M., 1955– . • Alternative energy sources / Kathiann M. Kowalski.
p. cm.— (Controversy!). • Includes bibliographical references and index.
ISBN 978-0-7614-4899-0
1. Renewable energy sources—Juvenile literature. I. Title.
TJ808.2.K69 2010. • 333.79'4—dc22 • 2009033402

Publisher: Michelle Bisson • Art Director: Anahid Hamparian
Series Designer: Alicia Mikles • Photo research by Lindsay Aveilhe

The photographs in this book are used by permission and through the courtesy of: Gary Gay/Getty Images: cover; Time & Life Pictures/Getty Images: 4; Lawrence Bender Prods./The Kobal Collection: 15; Reza/National Geographic/Getty Images: 22; Steve McCurry/Magnum Photos: 24; Lewis W. Hine/George Eastman House/Getty Images: 38; Phil Schermeister/Corbis: 40; Denis Poroy/AP Images: 51; Brooks Kraft/Corbis: 56; Tom Raymond/Getty Images: 64; Igor Kostin/Sygma/Corbis: 71; Rich Frishman/Getty Images: 73; John Locher-Pool/Getty Images: 81; Joe Mamer Photography/Alamy: 86; Steve Prezant/Corbis: 92; Steven Senne/AP Images: 97; Roderick Chen/Getty Images: 103; Robert Galbraith/Reuters: 108; Vincent Laforet/The New York Times: 113; David Sacks/Getty Images: 116.

Printed in Malaysia (T)

135642

Contents

In 1973 and 1974, the United States faced its worst gas shortage in history when Middle Eastern oil companies enforced a temporary embargo. By January 1974, it was so bad that some gas stations operated on an "appointment only" basis.

1 Why Alternative Energy?

IS THE UNITED STATES FACING AN ENERGY CRISIS? Many leading politicians and scientists say the country needs to make big changes in its energy policy. Some worry about environmental issues. Others worry about having an adequate supply at reasonable prices. Still others feel concerned about energy's role in the country's security. The majority of Americans agree that energy is a pressing issue.

In a 2009 survey by the Pew Research Center for the People & the Press, 60 percent of respondents named energy as a top priority for action by President Obama and Congress. Only the economy, jobs, terrorism, social security, and education ranked higher. In another survey by the Chicago Council on Global Affairs, 72 percent of respondents named a possible disruption in energy supply as a top critical threat to the United States' vital interests.

Having enough energy and being able to pay for it are huge challenges. The Energy Information Administration predicts that by 2030, worldwide energy consumption will be 44 percent greater than it was in 2006. The projected requirement of 678 quadrillion Btu's includes both transportation fuel and electricity usage. (Btu stands for British thermal unit, a standardized measure of heat energy.)

Sustainability is a big concern. Renewable sources still account for only a minority of the United States' energy. Other sources, such as fossil fuels and nuclear fuel, are limited in supply. Some energy sources also present serious environmental concerns.

Pain at the Pumps

Price plays a big role in people's perspectives on energy use. Consider how people reacted to the record gasoline prices in 2008. In July of 2008 the nationwide average price for gasoline was more than $4 per gallon. In September, Hurricane Ike hit Texas, shutting down one-fifth of the United States' oil-refining capacity. With fewer refineries to convert oil into gasoline, fuel prices surged to almost $5 per gallon in some areas of the United States.

Prices in some foreign countries were even higher. Demand for oil was increasing in large developing nations, such as China and India. When supply doesn't keep up with demand, prices rise. Suppliers sometimes cut back on production, too, in order to push prices higher and boost their profits.

Forecasts show that worldwide energy demand will continue to grow much more quickly than new oil reserves. "An oil crisis is coming—in the next 10 years," predicts John Hess, chair of Hess Corporation, a medium-size oil company. Once oil production reaches a maximum or peak, finding additional supplies becomes increasingly difficult, and prices increase as a result.

Even before gasoline prices reached record highs, politicians pressed for change. "Gas prices are killing folks," Democratic presidential candidate Barack Obama said in 2008. He wanted to reduce prices by cutting petroleum companies' profits.

Obama's Republican opponent, John McCain, wanted to institute a "tax holiday" to temporarily lower gas prices, in addition to increasing oil drilling. "Long-term," McCain added, "we've got to become used to nuclear, wind, solar, tide, all of the alternative energy, including a battery that will take a car 100 miles or 200 miles" before recharging.

Gasoline prices fell in late 2008 when a financial crisis, stock market problems, and other factors sparked a serious recession in the United States and elsewhere. Despite the price drop, President-elect Obama said he would still press for the development of alternative energy.

"It may be a little harder politically," Obama acknowledged in an interview on CBS's *60 Minutes*, "but it's more important." In his view the United States could not continue its "shock to trance" pattern of going from worrying about energy when prices were high to doing nothing after price hikes eased. The country's "addiction" to fossil fuels "has to be broken," Obama said.

Seeking Security

The United States learned it couldn't always count on imported oil when the Organization of the Petroleum Exporting Countries (OPEC) imposed a short-term oil embargo from 1973 to 1974. OPEC was angry about the United States' foreign-policy position on Israel. As a result, its member states temporarily stopped shipping crude oil to the United States and certain other countries. Long lines formed at gas stations, and gasoline prices increased fourfold.

In 1977 President Jimmy Carter proposed an ambitious policy program to buttress the United States' energy independence. "Now we have a choice," Carter said. "But if we wait, we will live in fear of embargoes. We could endanger our freedom as a sovereign nation to act in foreign affairs."

Because of Carter's initiative, the government set up the U.S. Strategic Petroleum Reserve. Government programs also funded more research on solar power and other technologies. However, the country did not commit to replacing fossil fuels with other energy sources. Because supplies from the Middle East had resumed, many people felt energy was not a priority. Due to economic problems and other issues, Carter lost his 1980 bid for reelection.

Now the United States has grown more dependent than ever on foreign energy resources. Back in 1970 the United States imported roughly 24 percent of its oil. By 2007 about 58 percent of its petroleum came from foreign sources. The United States still imports about two-thirds of the crude oil run through its refineries.

Canada and Mexico have consistently been among the top three sources of imported oil, and both countries have generally had friendly relationships with the United States. However, the United States has had tense political relationships with other countries that it relies on for millions of barrels of oil, including Venezuela and Russia.

Meanwhile, some Arab countries remain major producers of petroleum, and relationships with them continue to be tense. Saudi Arabia consistently ranks among the top three sources for imported petroleum. Kuwait, Iraq, and other countries in the region also supply significant amounts. Iran also has significant petroleum resources, yet it does not export to the United States because the two countries have not had a friendly diplomatic relationship for decades.

At the same time, petroleum-producing countries have grown less dependent on the United States' market and goodwill. China, India, and other developing nations are competing for a bigger share of the world's oil supplies. Thus, Sudan has found a ready market for its oil in China, despite U.S. economic sanctions imposed in response to the genocide and atrocities committed in Sudan's Darfur region.

With so many bad or fragile relationships, President George W. Bush called for greater energy independence and a move toward alternative energy. "America is addicted to oil, which is often imported from unstable parts of the world," Bush said in his 2006 State of the Union address. Both major-party candidates echoed the need for energy independence during the 2008 presidential campaign. "We've got to stop sending $700 billion a year to countries that don't like us very much," urged McCain.

Obama agreed that energy independence was a priority. "[W]e can't simply drill our way out of the problem," Obama said. "What we're going to have to do is to approach it through alternative energy, like solar, and wind, and biodiesel, and, yes, nuclear energy, clean-coal technology."

The world soon saw how insecure foreign energy supplies could be. In January 2009 Gazprom, Russia's government-owned natural gas company, stopped sending gas to Ukraine. Gazprom and Ukraine had arguments about overdue bills and a proposed price hike. Ukraine responded by not allowing natural gas to flow through pipelines within its borders to other countries. That action cut off most natural gas supplies to several Western European countries for more than a week.

The Gazprom dispute literally left Western Europe out in the cold. Policy makers don't want anything like that to happen to the United States.

Coping with Climate Change

For some people global climate change is the most compelling reason to switch to alternative energy sources. "Warming of the climate system is unequivocal," the Intergovernmental Panel on Climate Change (IPCC) reported in 2007. According to the IPCC, emissions of carbon dioxide and other compounds (collectively called greenhouse gases) that resulted from human activities very likely caused most of the increase in global average temperature since the mid-twentieth century. Carbon dioxide is the main greenhouse gas identified, along with methane and nitrous oxide. As of 2007 almost 57 percent of global carbon dioxide emissions came from burning fossil fuels, including coal, petroleum, and natural gas. Among those fossil fuels, coal produces the most carbon dioxide emissions.

Throughout the twenty-first century average global temperatures will continue to increase anywhere from 2 to 11.5 degrees Fahrenheit (1.1 to 6.4 degrees Celsius). Average temperature increases will be greater if greenhouse gas emissions continue to

U.S. Energy Consumption by Source, 2007

Fossil fuels are the primary sources of energy used in the United States.

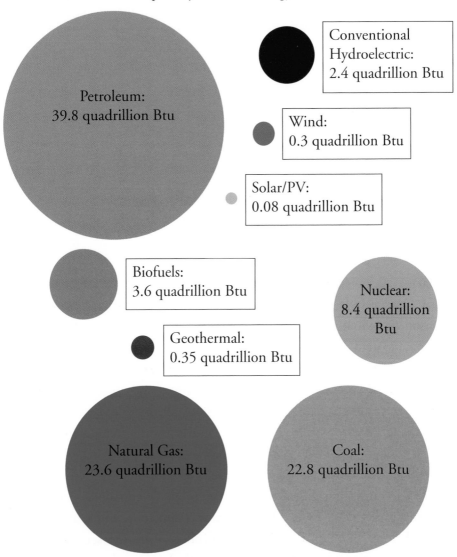

Conventional
Hydroelectric:
2.4 quadrillion Btu

Petroleum:
39.8 quadrillion Btu

Wind:
0.3 quadrillion Btu

Solar/PV:
0.08 quadrillion Btu

Biofuels:
3.6 quadrillion Btu

Nuclear:
8.4 quadrillion
Btu

Geothermal:
0.35 quadrillion Btu

Natural Gas:
23.6 quadrillion Btu

Coal:
22.8 quadrillion Btu

Source: Energy Information Administration, "U.S. Energy Consumption by Energy Source—Data for: 2007," Release date, April 2009, http://www.eia.doe.gov/cneaf/solar.renewables/page/trends/table1.html. Total U.S. energy consumption for 2007 was 101,545 quadrillion Btu, including coal coke net imports and electricity net imports. Balloons not shown for coal coke and electricity net imports or for energy sources less than 0.08 quadrillion Btu.
Graphic created by author.

increase. The temperature increases may not sound like a lot. However, climate scientists warn that even such slight changes can have serious effects.

One problem is that higher average temperatures increase the chances that extreme weather events, such as droughts or hurricanes, will take place. Warming of a few degrees can also cause some ice to melt in polar regions, which would release enough water to make sea levels rise. Catastrophic weather events and flooding in coastal areas would cause widespread economic loss. Other impacts would include loss of life from accidents or illness related to severe weather events, as well as increased rates of various diseases in the aftermath of natural disasters. Ecosystems would also undergo changes, including damage to coral reefs and shifts in prevailing species in land environments.

"We don't know exactly how serious the effects will be," noted Mark Levine at the Environmental Energy Technologies Division of Lawrence Berkeley National Laboratory. Nonetheless, "The potential for climate change to cause very, very, very serious impacts is quite high."

The IPCC has called for mitigation measures—steps to control and reduce greenhouse gas emissions in order to avoid the worst effects of climate change. In the short term the IPCC wants countries to improve energy efficiency. Ideally, such measures would allow time to develop and use alternative energy sources.

As is true with many other issues, the scientific community lacks consensus on the extent and causes of global climate change. Earth has experienced periods of global warming and cooling since long before the Industrial Revolution. The nature of scientific studies prevents people from saying exactly how much observed and predicted climate change is the result of human activities versus natural cycles. Also, scientists cannot say that human impact on climate definitely caused any single climate event, such as Hurricane Katrina in 2005.

Electricity 101

Basically, electricity is the flow of positive and negative charges through atoms in the form of a current. In a typical power plant generator an electromagnet—a magnet formed by the flow of electrical current, as opposed to a naturally occurring, permanent magnet—spins at high speeds within coils of wire. The spinning electromagnet generates electricity. Electricity flows from the generator through wires and out to users through a system called the grid.

Getting the electromagnet to spin can be done in different ways. A steam turbine uses the steam from boiling water to turn the blades of an electric generator. The generator's spinning blades make the electromagnet rotate to produce electricity.

To make the steam, fossil fuel plants burn coal, oil, or natural gas to boil water. Biofuel plants burn other forms of fuel, such as plant matter. Nuclear plants use the heat energy created by a controlled chain reaction to boil water. Solar concentration facilities do the job with heat from concentrated sunlight.

Other types of power plants skip the step of boiling water. Instead, they move other fluids through a turbine's blades. Hydroelectric power plants rely on flowing water to power their turbines. Wind turbines use the force of air currents in the form of wind to rotate them. (A fluid can be either a liquid or a gas.)

Photovoltaic cells (PV cells or solar cells) do not use a turbine at all. The cells convert light energy directly to electricity.

Nevertheless, the majority of scientists now support the consensus represented by the IPCC's latest reports. Likewise, many policy makers accept that climate change is a real concern. Disputes remain about what actions the nation should take in response and how much of its resources should go toward addressing the issue.

Within the United States the strongest political call for action on climate change has come from former vice president Al Gore. His 2006 film *An Inconvenient Truth* highlighted possible dangers if governments worldwide do not take swift action to cut greenhouse gas emissions, including carbon dioxide. Critics claimed that the film was alarmist, yet the movie won an Academy Award for best documentary. More significantly, Gore and the IPCC shared the 2007 Nobel Peace Prize for their efforts to inform and educate the world about climate change and its impacts.

Gore's Nobel acceptance speech highlighted the threats of climate change and the need for immediate action.

> We, the human species, are confronting a planetary emergency—a threat to the survival of our civilization that is gathering ominous and destructive potential even as we gather here. But there is hopeful news as well: We have the ability to solve this crisis and avoid the worst—though not all—of its consequences, if we act boldly, decisively and quickly.

Because climate change does not happen solely within any country's borders, proposed responses call for international action. The Kyoto Protocol is a treaty agreement that was added to the United Nations Framework Convention on Climate Change. It called for industrialized countries to reduce greenhouse gas emissions by up to 8 percent from 1990 levels. By late 2009, 189 countries had formally accepted its terms.

Some countries are cutting back on their own greenhouse gas emissions. Others are using the treaty's emissions trading mechanism. In effect, the trading mechanism lets countries continue to emit higher levels of greenhouse gases if they arrange for decreases elsewhere. An example would be providing pollution-control mechanisms or lower-emissions technologies for use in a developing country that is not bound by the treaty's emissions limits. Building newer, more efficient facilities in other countries is sometimes cheaper than replacing or modifying equipment throughout an industrialized nation. And the end result is lower global emissions.

Although the United States signed the Kyoto Protocol in 1997, the country never ratified the treaty. The Senate passed a 95–0 resolution against the Kyoto Protocol in 1998, so President Clinton did not seek ratification.

President Bush announced in 2001 that he disagreed with the treaty and would not ask the Senate to ratify it. He felt that the treaty would put American products at a disadvantage in the international marketplace, compared with those from large developing countries that had no obligation to cut back emissions. "I will not accept a plan that will harm our economy and hurt American workers," Bush said.

In contrast, President Obama strongly supports curbs on greenhouse gas emissions. In early 2009, Obama asked Congress to pass a law restricting those emissions. In response, the House passed a bill to set up a cap-and-trade system. The government would set emissions limits for various sources of greenhouse gases. Companies that could not meet permit limits would either pay the government for the legal right to emit more carbon dioxide, or they could make private deals with other parties for their unused

Former vice president Al Gore's 2006 documentary, *An Inconvenient Truth*, served as a major eye-opener on the issue of climate change.

By far the most terrifying film you will ever see.

aninconvenienttruth
A GLOBAL WARNING

but allowed emissions. Legislation was still pending in the Senate as this book went to press. The government will need to issue regulations to implement whatever climate change law Congress ultimately passes.

Meanwhile, the Kyoto Protocol's limits will end in 2012. In December 2009, the world's countries held a summit meeting in Copenhagen, Denmark, to discuss the next steps. No new treaty limits resulted from that meeting. However, the United States and other industrialized nations agreed in principle to help poorer countries curb greenhouse gases through alternative energy and other technologies. Aid provided by the richer countries would come from public and private sources. The amount could total $100 billion annually by 2020.

Further meetings will take place to explore binding emission limits among countries. Smaller groups of nations may also agree to binding limits among themselves. In any case, the United States is moving forward.

Shortly before the Copenhagen conference, the Obama administration announced that by 2020, the United States plans to cut greenhouse gas emissions by 17 percent, compared to 2005 levels. That statement was in line with the pending legislation. According to the White House statement, additional actions would achieve an 83 percent reduction in emissions by 2050.

Even if Congress did not pass any specific climate change law, a 2007 Supreme Court ruling held that the Environmental Protection Agency already has authority to regulate greenhouse gases. In December 2009, the Environmental Protection Agency made a formal finding that greenhouse gas emissions threaten the public health and welfare. A companion finding paved the way for agency rules on greenhouse gas emissions from new motor vehicles. Future findings will likely target other industries.

One way or another, then, laws and regulations will require

various companies to cut back emissions of greenhouse gases or else pay extra—either in fines, by fees for private deals to offset emissions, or through other arrangements. Companies will have more incentives to use alternative energy sources. They will also pay more for energy from coal and petroleum than they have in the past. Both results will support shifts to alternative energy.

Green Sector Growth

Desire for economic growth is another factor fueling the push for alternative energy. Over the last several decades the United States has lost millions of manufacturing jobs. Factory automation and other technological advances eliminated many jobs. Many companies also chose to close some facilities in the United States. Sometimes foreign competition became too tough. Other times companies chose to locate facilities and jobs in countries with lower costs and lower prevailing wages. Many service-sector jobs have also been eliminated, as some countries have chosen to "outsource" work abroad. For example, instead of having telephone service representatives work in the United States, companies may rely on English-speaking workers living in foreign countries.

Even more job losses came after the financial crisis in 2008 and the related economic downturn. By August 2009, 14.9 million people were out of work. More than one-third of them had been out of work for more than six months.

No single strategy or policy will provide a surefire cure for the country's economic problems. Nevertheless, advocates of alternative energy say its development can help spur economic recovery. Obama himself announced a goal of creating 5 million new jobs. To bring about that growth, Obama called for $150 billion of investments over a ten-year period. Other groups have likewise urged investments to promote "green collar" jobs—including work that provides environmentally friendly renewable energy.

The World Energy Outlook

The United States isn't the only country facing a potential energy crisis. The International Energy Agency (IEA), an agency within the Organisation for Economic Co-operation and Development (OECD), reports that the world must take action now to develop alternative energy technologies and improve efficiency. Otherwise, the IEA's *World Energy Outlook 2008* concluded, the world won't be able to meet its growing energy demands. As Nobuo Tanaka, executive director of the International Energy Agency, put it:

> We must usher in a global energy revolution by improving energy efficiency and increasing the deployment of low-carbon energy. . . .
>
> Current trends in energy supply and consumption are patently unsustainable—environmentally, economically and socially. They can and must be altered.

Analysts vary widely in their projections of potential growth in this field. At one extreme CRA International, a consulting firm that has worked with the coal industry, has suggested that job losses in other sectors of the economy will offset any green collar gains. Other observers are more optimistic.

Reports from the Natural Resources Defense Council (NRDC), the Center for American Progress, Green for All, and the University of Massachusetts' Political Economy Research Institute estimate that a $150 billion investment could create a net increase of 1.7 million American jobs. "Net" means the difference between total job gains and any losses resulting from shifts away from other fields. "It's never been clearer that American ingenuity and investment in clean energy can be a driving force for economic growth, energy independence, and environmental protection," said NRDC executive director Peter Lehner, "so we can increase economic opportunities while reducing global warming pollution."

While the numbers remain open to debate, the appeal of creating jobs remains. Meanwhile, the United States continues to face stiff foreign competition for various products and services. President Obama summed up these sentiments for supporting alternative energy:

> We can remain one of the world's leading importers of foreign oil, or we can make the investments that would allow us to become the world's leading exporter of renewable energy. . . . We can let the jobs of tomorrow be created abroad, or we can create those jobs right here in America and lay the foundation for our lasting prosperity.

No Magic Wand

It's one thing to call for the expanded use of alternatives to fossil fuel. It's another thing to make it happen in a way that will be reliable and practical. Technologies also need to be able to supply enough energy to deal with growing demand. Otherwise, the United States and other countries could face problems sustaining economic growth.

Conservation measures are one way to keep growing energy demand in check. Energy demand and usage will still increase, but conservation can slow the rate of growth. Besides saving money, conservation can buy time for scientists and policy makers to develop more alternative energy choices for consumers and businesses. Energy-saving measures can also help deal with other issues relating to energy usage, such as greenhouse gas emissions and climate change. Nonetheless, conservation strategies will not solve all of America's or the world's energy problems. Thus, alternative energy projects will continue to grow and develop.

Technologies like nuclear power and hydroelectric power have been providing energy for decades. However, people differ widely on whether and how to expand those technologies. Other technologies are still mostly on the drawing board. Hydrogen fuel cell technology is one example. It is providing limited amounts of energy in some places. However, it's not at all certain when and whether that technology will become widespread.

Other technologies are further along, including biofuels, solar energy, and wind power, but they are only a small part of the country's energy mix. Meanwhile, supporters and critics debate how much energy they can realistically supply and how practical the technologies can be.

Policy makers will probably pursue a mix of energy options. Such a strategy avoids the risks of relying on any single technology. It allows more flexibility and may encourage greater innovation. It could also help maximize available energy resources by taking advantage of different regions' strengths.

Cost is an issue for all energy choices. If all else is equal, most buyers choose the option with the lowest price. To compete effectively, alternative energy costs should be close to those of other options.

For electricity, energy costs already vary with users' demand. "Base load" refers to round-the-clock energy demand for basic services and needs. "Peak" demand describes users' need for electricity during high-usage periods, such as warm summer afternoons, when homes and businesses are likely to be running air conditioners. An alternative energy option that might appear expensive for meeting base-load energy needs can become competitive when compared with choices for meeting peak electricity demands.

As technologies improve, rates for alternative energy will likely come down. Yet the expansion of any energy technology will require investments. Much of that money will probably come from the private sector. Lots of it will likely come from the government, too, in the form of grants, subsidies, or tax breaks for such investments. The public and consumers will ultimately pay, both through taxes and in the prices charged for electricity, transportation, and various products.

Of course, energy is not the only issue demanding public and private resources. Starting in late 2007, the U.S. economy suffered a severe recession, and Americans faced millions of layoffs. By August 2009 the unemployment rate had climbed to 9.7 percent. Millions of people had also suffered huge losses in the stock market, home mortgage foreclosures, and other problems. Meanwhile, lawmakers agreed to massive bailout programs for insurers, investment firms, banks, and some automakers.

At the same time the country remained in expensive wars in Afghanistan and Iraq. Health care reform also took center stage in the national forum, after President Obama followed up on his campaign promises by proposing a program of sweeping changes to Congress. All these and other interests compete for limited resources.

Different issues are also intertwined. Expanding alternative

The United States remains dependent on oil from foreign sources, such as Saudi Arabia and other Arab states.

energy supplies may well help jump-start the economy, as President Obama urged in his 2009 economic stimulus proposal. On the other hand, more downturns in the economy could dry up sources for some investments in alternative energy.

Doing nothing also comes with costs. Energy security, price, and limited supplies would remain concerns. Environmental issues would still exist. Also, even existing technologies would eventually require huge investments, as various facilities are near the end of their useful lives.

Keep these issues of costs and competing interests in mind when thinking about alternative energy. Try to evaluate options with an eye toward both short-term and long-term consequences. Ultimately, as a citizen, consumer, and taxpayer, you will be paying for the United States' energy choices in the coming years.

2 Fossil Fuels: The Status Quo

DESPITE ARGUMENTS FOR MOVING AWAY FROM fossil fuels, some people believe the country should continue to exploit those energy resources. Fossil fuels already supply the overwhelming majority of the United States' current energy needs. Petroleum products provide energy for most transportation purposes, with a small portion coming from electricity or other fuels. Coal-powered plants supply about half the country's electricity, with additional amounts coming from petroleum and natural gas plants.

Ancient Energy

Most deposits of coal, petroleum, and natural gas began forming roughly 360 to 286 million years ago, during part of the Paleozoic Era called the Carboniferous Period. Trees, ferns, and other plants covered large, swampy areas on land. Algae and seaweed thrived in the oceans.

Normally when plants and algae die, the decay process releases compounds back into the environment. During the Carboniferous Period, however, low-oxygen conditions at the bottom of prehistoric swamps and oceans significantly slowed the decay process. The remains built up into layers called peat.

The use of oil has many supporters, but a bird covered by oil from a spill off the coast of Saudi Arabia would not be among them.

Over thousands of years sand and other materials formed rock layers over the peat. Pressure from the overlying rock eventually squeezed out any remaining moisture. Depending on the local conditions, the buried material became coal, petroleum, or natural gas. Burning coal, petroleum, or natural gas releases energy that has been stored in chemical bonds for millions of years.

"Drill, Baby, Drill!"

"Drill, baby, drill!" The chant echoed through St. Paul's Xcel Energy Center at the Republican National Convention in 2008. Supporters echoed the refrain at McCain-Palin campaign rallies throughout fall 2008. While the Republican presidential and vice presidential candidates called for an increase in the production of alternative energy, they also wanted to increase oil exploration on public lands and offshore. Obama felt that drilling for more fossil fuels in U.S. territory was only a stopgap measure, yet he too called on oil companies to exploit existing oil leases. As a political matter, neither political party wanted to be blamed for higher gasoline prices.

Typically, petroleum and natural gas occur together, with the less dense natural gas sitting on top of petroleum deposits. Drilling is the main method for getting both petroleum and natural gas out of the ground. Until the late twentieth century most petroleum drilling took place on land. Since then, offshore oil exploration and drilling have expanded.

Natural gas is mostly methane, a gas made of molecules with a carbon atom bonded to four hydrogen atoms. Burning natural gas produces carbon dioxide as a waste product, which is a greenhouse gas. However, the Union of Concerned Scientists reports that natural gas use emits 30 percent less carbon dioxide than petroleum and 43 percent less than coal. For particulates, natural gas's emissions are one-twelfth those of petroleum and less than one percent of coal. Natural gas emissions of carbon monoxide, sulfur dioxide, and other pollutants are also dramatically lower.

As of 2007 natural gas supplied roughly 22 percent of the United States' energy needs. Natural gas powers some electricity-generating plants. Another major use is for home and industrial heating. More than half the nation's homes currently use natural gas as their main heating fuel.

Petroleum, also called crude oil, is a mixture of complex, long-chain molecules called hydrocarbons. Molecules in the mixture have varying arrangements of carbon, hydrogen, and other atoms. Refineries separate crude oil into its various parts, or fractions, by heating it to high temperatures inside a tall column, called a distillation column. As lighter parts boil and change to a gas, they separate from the mixture. Petroleum refining produces the products we know as gasoline, diesel fuel, and jet fuel. It also produces home heating oil, raw materials for the chemical and plastics industries, road-paving products, and other materials.

Experts debate just how extensive the world's petroleum resources are. Part of the uncertainty comes from variations in whether and how fully different countries report on their estimated reserves. Changes in exploration and recovery techniques could also affect how much petroleum is available. Currently, conventionally drilled oil is significantly cheaper to get and process than is oil extracted from shale, oil sands, or other sources.

One study from Sweden's Uppsala University estimated that world oil production could start declining soon after 2010. After any peak, the British Broadcasting Corporation (BBC) reported, the world could have anywhere from forty to one hundred years of oil left. A more optimistic view came from Cambridge Energy Research Associates, in Massachusetts. It estimated that petroleum reserves could easily produce more than 100 million barrels of crude oil daily by 2017—up from the 2008 level of 85 million barrels per day.

Polls in 2008 showed roughly 70 percent of the American public supported expanded drilling for petroleum. Even after economic setbacks caused gasoline prices to drop, a 2009 Harris Interactive poll found that 61 percent of voters wanted more offshore oil and gas drilling.

Republican Newt Gingrich, a former speaker of the house and vocal conservative politician, has argued that restrictions on offshore oil drilling and drilling in Alaska, as well as other policies, have created an "artificial energy crisis." His claim appears to rest on a classic economic assumption that limiting supply tends to drive up prices.

Critics contend that increased drilling would have little impact on energy prices. One 2004 study concluded that drilling in the Arctic National Wildlife Refuge might slash gasoline prices by 3.5 cents per gallon—by 2027. Meanwhile, the United States' energy consumption remains high. Demand from China, India, and other countries is also increasing. Even the extraction of 75 billion barrels of oil from the Arctic area would be just "a drop in the bucket," reported Environmental Defense Fund economist Gernot Wagner.

Nevertheless, current transportation technology depends heavily on petroleum products and will do so for several decades. According to the Energy Information Administration, oil and gas will still supply half of the United States' energy needs in 2030.

"What the nation needs is a policy that increases, not decreases, domestic energy production," Larry Nichols, chair of the American Petroleum Institute (API), said in 2009. Of course, the industry has a strong profit interest in increased oil and gas drilling.

Critics counter that any benefits from added drilling would be temporary. The sooner the United States breaks its dependence on fossil fuels, they argue, the better. In these critics' view the country would do best to develop alternative energy sources now instead of pushing the problem onto future generations.

Environmental worries come into play too. The API argues that the environmental and safety record for offshore drilling is "second to none." However, critics worry about the potential for an oil spill harming the ocean environment. In 1989 the *Exxon Valdez* oil tanker spilled approximately 11 million gallons of oil into Prince William Sound, south of Alaska. The spill polluted approximately 1,300 miles of coastline. Oil tankers have put multiple safeguards in place since then, but spills remain a concern.

Various critics also oppose oil drilling in wilderness areas. Even though many Americans support increased oil and gas exploration, 55 percent of people questioned in a 2008 poll still opposed drilling in the Arctic National Wildlife Refuge.

Debate will continue over expanded oil and gas drilling both on and offshore. However, efforts to expand drilling would not prohibit the development of alternative energy resources. "Oil and natural gas are the indispensable bridge to anyone's projected realization of an alternative fuels future," API president Red Cavaney argued in 2007. Indeed, some traditional petroleum companies have already invested heavily in alternative energy technologies. For example, BP has become a leading producer of solar energy equipment.

Old King Coal

As of 2009 coal produced approximately half of the United States' electricity. The coal industry has a strong financial interest in having coal continue to be a big part of the United States' energy mix.

Coal is a black, solid material that contains carbon, hydrogen, oxygen, nitrogen, and sulfur. Depending on its hardness and energy content, coal falls into four general categories: lignite, sub-bituminous coal, bituminous coal, and anthracite. About half of the United States' coal production is bituminous coal, with a carbon content between 45 and 86 percent. Another 44 percent is sub-bituminous coal, which is 35 to 45 percent carbon.

Archaeologists trace humans' use of coal for energy back more than three thousand years. Since the Industrial Revolution began, coal's use has skyrocketed. Coal has provided relatively cheap power for steel plants, factories, and other industrial facilities. Starting in the 1950s, coal's primary use shifted from powering factories to generating electricity. Basically, a coal-fired electrical plant burns coal. Heat from that process creates steam, which turns turbines and generates electricity.

Historically, coal's market price has been relatively low. However, coal's real costs have not always been reflected in the prices people pay for it. For one thing, coal mining has long been an inherently dangerous job. Workers face constant threats of cave-ins or other accidents. The backbreaking work has also left many workers with health problems, such as black lung disease. In the United States the law did not require safeguards or even compensation for these problems until well into the twentieth century. Policies vary in other countries, with some providing little or no benefits for injured workers.

Coal has caused environmental problems too. Surface mining often leaves the land scarred and barren. Also, chemicals left in the ground react with rainwater to pollute farmlands and waterways. Failure to close a deep mine properly also causes acid to drain from the mine.

Burning coal produces more pollution. For example, the nitrogen oxide and sulfur dioxide it releases can both cause serious breathing ailments. Those pollutants also add to problems such as acid rain, which damages soils, plant life, and waterways. Coal burning also emits particulates—tiny bits of pollutants that aggravate asthma and other breathing problems.

The U.S. government has regulated the release of these and other pollutants since the 1970s. However, older coal plants remain a concern for groups like the Sierra Club, which argues that they are dirtier and more polluting. Environmental groups continue to press for stricter pollution limits.

More recently, greenhouse gas emissions have become a concern. Coal-powered plants release huge amounts of carbon dioxide

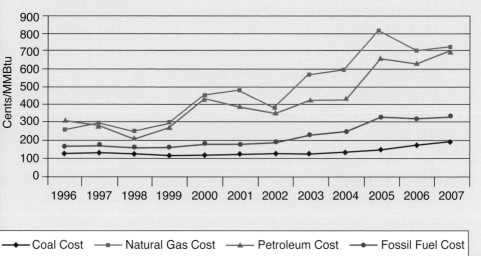

Fuel Costs for Electricity Generation, 1996–2007

Source: Energy Information Administration, "Figure ES4. Fuel Costs for the Electricity Generation," released January 21, 2009. http//:www.eia.doe.gov/cneaf/electricity/epa/figes4.html (accessed September 8, 2009).

Among fossil fuel sources, coal has generally had the cheapest cost per unit of electricity generation. The chart reflects amounts paid for producing electricity, but not impacts on the atmosphere or other consequences for which utilities have not previously borne the costs.

into the atmosphere. This worries people who are concerned about climate change.

Taking steps to prevent or lower carbon dioxide emissions could eliminate much of the price advantage coal has had over other energy resources. Until stricter requirements become mandatory, though, cost continues to be a big advantage for coal.

Improvements in efficiency could also lower pollution levels, because they would require that less coal be burned per unit of electricity produced. The average efficiency of coal-fired power plants worldwide is approximately 30 percent. That means 70 percent of the energy released from the coal as heat goes to waste. The most advanced plants in the United States are still only about 40 percent efficient. In contrast, China now has some plants that achieve 44 percent efficiency, and the German company Siemens AG has announced plans for a high-temperature coal-powered plant that will be at least 50 percent efficient. In short, there is room to improve efficiency if companies are willing to invest in new plants and if the electricity rates will repay those investments over time.

Clean Coal?

Coal's other big advantage is that there's a lot of it. At current usage rates, the United States has enough coal to last at least two hundred years. Industry supporters say coal can help provide energy security. At a minimum, they say, the United States should invest in clean-coal technologies.

"It is imperative that we figure out a way to use coal as cleanly as possible," agreed Secretary of Energy Steven Chu at his confirmation hearing in 2009. Since 1986 the Department of Energy has funded research on how to reduce pollution from coal. The first projects targeted the problem of acid rain—a change in rainwater quality linked to sulfur and nitrogen compounds emitted from coal-burning power plants. Current pollution-control efforts seek to reduce the emission of mercury compounds and particulate matter.

Starting in 2008, the Department of Energy's Clean Coal Power Initiative announced funding for research projects on ways to capture or use carbon dioxide emissions from coal-burning power plants. One idea is to capture carbon dioxide emissions before they enter the atmosphere. Possible uses for the carbon dioxide might include the manufacture of carbonated beverages and so-called dry ice for portable refrigeration. Carbon dioxide is also useful in

China's Energy Outlook

As China's economy has expanded over the last twenty years, the number of coal-fired power plants in that country has grown dramatically. In recent years China has added an average of two large coal power plants each week. "More than 70 percent of our power generation and total energy capacity is from the coal," embassy spokesperson Ma Amin reported in 2007.

Carbon dioxide from coal-fired power plants and gases from steel mills, concrete plants, and other heavy industries have made China the world's leading greenhouse gas emitter. Until 2008 the United States held that position. However, the two countries' situations differ in important respects.

"As a developing country, people's living standards are still quite low compared to here in the U.S.," Ma noted. "And our per capita energy consumption is also quite low." As of 2007, 20 million Chinese people still had no electric power in their homes.

While coal continues to play a big role in China's electricity production, the country is also embracing alternative energy technologies. By 2020 China hopes that 15 percent of its energy will come from renewable sources, such as wind power, hydroelectric power, solar energy, and biofuels. China is also expanding its nuclear energy capacity.

China is already emerging as a global trade leader in alternative energy equipment. China is one of the largest producers of photovoltaic cells, with exports going to countries around the world.

pneumatic systems, fire extinguishers, and other applications. However, consumer and industrial applications would not use all the carbon dioxide produced by coal-burning power plants.

The alternative to reusing carbon dioxide is to sequester the gas, or store it away somewhere, for thousands of years. Depleted oil and gas wells could provide a place to put carbon dioxide. Oil companies already pump limited amounts of carbon dioxide into wells to maintain pressure and force out more oil and natural gas. "If we've got the oil and gas in these depleted fields and we can get it out while sequestering carbon at the same time, that's a win-win," said Department of Energy spokesman John Grasser in 2008. The oil companies would increase productivity, and carbon dioxide emissions would decrease.

Even if oil and gas fields are no longer productive, they could still provide huge storage areas for carbon dioxide. One pilot plant in Germany converts waste carbon dioxide gas into a liquid under high pressure and then stores it at −18 °F. Trucks take the liquefied carbon dioxide approximately 100 miles to a depleted natural gas field, where it is then pumped underground. The plant, run by the Swedish company Vattenfall, was hailed in early 2009 as the world's first clean coal plant. However, the technology is not yet in place anywhere on a full-scale commercial basis.

Deep saline aquifers are another possible place to sequester carbon dioxide. An aquifer is a layer of rock or soil that holds fluids in its pores. Deep-well injection into aquifers is already used for the disposal of some wastes, such as those from making acrylics.

Yet another possible storage place for carbon dioxide might be deep in the oceans. At the high pressure found deep underwater, the gas would dissolve. However, altering the oceans' carbon dioxide levels could cause serious environmental problems. If the dissolved gas made the water more acidic, it might harm aquatic species and their habitats. Alternatively, putting greater amounts of carbon dioxide into the ocean could spur the growth of various organisms that would overwhelm other species or deplete available oxygen supplies.

Any large-scale carbon sequestration program would eventually need a way to transport carbon dioxide to its target locations. It would require a new network of underground pipelines or huge fleets of tanker trucks that would take liquefied gas from coal-burning power plants to sequestration locations. Either approach would require massive investments. Both would also require energy to implement, thus limiting the total reduction in greenhouse gas emissions.

Then there is the size of the problem. Within the United States coal-burning power plants generate nearly 2 billion tons of carbon dioxide per year. Finding places to put all of it would be a massive task.

Coal gasification could reduce the total amount of carbon dioxide being handled. Basically, the power plant would subject coal to a process that converts it into the functional equivalent of natural gas. The plant would then burn that gas to generate electricity. Supporters say that the result would be lower emissions of carbon dioxide and other pollutants. Even without carbon capture and storage technologies, coal gasification could significantly curb pollution problems. However, making the process into standard practice would incur substantial costs.

Some critics worry about what would happen if something went wrong with a carbon capture and storage project. In 1986 a huge carbon dioxide plume erupted from Lake Nyos, a volcanic crater lake in Cameroon. The carbon dioxide displaced the normal air in the surrounding area, and about 1,700 people died from asphyxiation. They couldn't get enough free oxygen to breathe. The Lake Nyos event occurred naturally. *IEEE Spectrum* editor William Sweet has suggested that similar catastrophes could occur if carbon dioxide were to escape from underground storage areas.

Other critics of sequestration, such as the Union of Concerned

Scientists, suggest that leaking carbon dioxide could contaminate water supplies by making them acidic. More seriously, the group argues, leaks of stored carbon dioxide could increase greenhouse gases and worsen climate change, negating any benefits of deep burial.

A more optimistic scenario suggests that deeply buried carbon dioxide would cause few problems. Because carbon dioxide dissolves in water, deep groundwater supplies below the water table might trap up to 90 percent in solution. Some of that sparkling water might eventually bubble up to the surface. However, it would be a slow, mostly harmless process, probably similar to the process that produces natural cold-water geysers. In this scenario, most of the carbon dioxide would remain buried deep in the earth.

Yet another strategy for making fossil fuels a cleaner energy source is to find new ways to recycle carbon dioxide. Scientists at Sandia National Laboratories have been exploring ways to convert carbon dioxide into methanol, which can be used as fuel. Similar research is under way at Carbon Sciences, a private company that hopes to profit eventually from its carbon-dioxide-to-fuel work.

Successful technologies could let the United States and other countries keep using their plentiful coal resources for energy without worsening environmental problems. However, it's unclear when the industry could use those technologies widely. In one 2008 report the consulting firm McKinsey & Company looked at the potential for implementation of carbon dioxide capture-and-storage systems in the European Union. At best, it concluded, substantial use of such methods by 2030 was questionable.

Meanwhile, global greenhouse gas emissions keep mounting. Also, if and when the industry adopts new technologies on a widespread basis, it will pass on any added costs to consumers in the form of higher rates. Under those circumstances, coal energy's price tag for users could be considerably higher than it is now. Indeed, critics say, it could exceed prices for other forms of energy that are already cleaner and renewable, such as solar energy or wind power.

Critics portray industry efforts touting clean coal as just a public relations campaign to dupe consumers. At a minimum, they say, arguments over clean coal divert resources from more promising alternative energy strategies. At worst, they call it downright misleading.

"There is no such thing as clean coal," insists James Hansen, an expert on climate change with the National Aeronautics and Space Administration (NASA). Even the newest commercial coal-fired power plants continue to emit great amounts of carbon dioxide and other pollutants. The Reality Coalition, an alliance of various environmental groups, echoed that conclusion in a 2008 ad campaign.

"The technology is feasible," admits Hansen, "but there's not real incentive to do it, because neither the coal companies nor the utilities really want it. They'd prefer to use the coal in the cheapest way possible." Hansen has also questioned the government's political commitment to clean-coal projects.

In 2003 the Department of Energy announced the FutureGen Industrial Alliance—an effort to develop a near-zero-emissions power plant that combined coal gasification with the capture and storage of carbon dioxide. The pilot power plant was to operate in Mattoon, Illinois. Just five years later the government withdrew from the Future-Gen Alliance. Apparently, the problem was money. By that time, costs for the unfinished project were already $1.8 billion.

FutureGen "should have been called NeverGen," Hansen has argued. "It was just an example of 'greenwash,'" he explained, "where the government said we're working on clean coal, but in fact they never completed the plant."

Other critics stress that carbon dioxide emissions are not the only problem with coal. "Even if coal capture and storage works on

a commercial scale, coal will still be dirty," Steve Clemmer of the Union of Concerned Scientists has argued. "The technology doesn't address the environmental threat posed by mining, transporting, and disposing of coal."

Such arguments have some sway in the political arena. Nonetheless, research on reducing and capturing coal emissions will likely continue. The industry has huge amounts invested in existing plants and other resources, and it heavily lobbies politicians of both major political parties. Various candidates don't want to turn away a source of campaign contributions. Other politicians do not want to shut down a large industry sector that employs many people.

Also, not everyone agrees that the United States should turn away from fossil fuels. Even if the country wanted to abandon them, practical factors would delay that for at least several decades.

This 1910 Pennsylvania coal miner would have been amazed at the notion of "clean coal."

Corn is is a major source for ethanol produced in the United States.

3 Biofuels

TELEVISION VIEWERS LAUGHED WHEN GRANNY gassed up her jalopy truck with moonshine in a 1968 episode of *The Beverly Hillbillies*. In the sitcom the high-alcohol White Lightning fuel let the feisty backwoods woman's truck race faster than her nephew's fancy new car.

Today's biofuels require more elaborate refining than Granny's fictional home brew did. Yet ethanol, which is the most common biofuel, is basically alcohol. (Added chemicals make ethanol fuel harmful if consumed, so never drink any biofuels!) The idea of using ethanol as fuel started long before the old sitcom. Henry Ford reportedly designed his 1908 Model T car to use either ethanol or gasoline.

Another type of biofuel is primarily vegetable oil. Using vegetable oil as fuel isn't a new idea either. An early diesel engine ran on peanut oil at the 1900 Paris Exhibition.

Biofuels are playing a growing role in transportation. Waste organic materials, or biomass, are also playing a part in electric power generation. In the Energy Independence and Security Act of 2007 the federal government stated that by 2022, it wants vehicles to use up to 36 billion gallons per year of biofuels. Up to 15 billion gallons per year would come from corn-based ethanol. The rest—up to 21 billion gallons per year—would come from other sources.

The government's emphasis on biofuels offers a way to reduce the nation's reliance on imported fossil fuels. The legislation also offers incentives to businesses to expand and develop new technologies, which might produce substantial profits. However, biofuel technologies present some issues of concern.

Ethanol—Fuel-wise or Foolish?

Ethanol made in the United States comes mainly from corn. Brazil makes most of its ethanol from sugarcane. Other crops can provide ethanol too. Whatever the source, the plant material yields ethanol through a process called yeast fermentation. Yeast cells eat sugars in the plant material; the amount of available sugars varies from crop to crop. Ethanol is a by-product of the process, as is carbon dioxide.

Biofuels got their first big boost in the late 1970s, after the Arab oil embargo raised concerns about America's energy policies. Because the United States can grow lots of corn and other crops, biofuels can reduce its reliance on foreign oil. Supporters say developing our biofuels is an important step toward energy independence for the United States.

Supporters say ethanol can also be more environmentally friendly than fossil fuels. Ethanol comes from plants, so it is renewable. After farmers harvest biofuel crops, more can grow. This reduces concerns about using up nonrenewable resources such as petroleum.

Supporters say that ethanol can reduce greenhouse gas emissions and curb climate change. Carbon dioxide does get released into the atmosphere when ethanol burns. But growing crops to make more ethanol removes carbon dioxide from the air. Waste products from burning ethanol also lack some trace pollutants found in gasoline, such as mercury and other nonbiodegradable compounds.

Politicians have promoted ethanol as an effective answer to America's energy problems. They have backed up that enthusiasm with laws that create and support a market for biofuels. For example, the Renewable Fuel Standards provision calls for biofuels to make up a certain percentage of motor vehicle fuels sold in the United States. In 2009 that requirement translated into a market for more than 11 billion gallons of ethanol. Under other federal rules refiners can no longer boost gasoline octane with a chemical called MBTE (methyl tertiary butyl ether). Ethanol can do the same job, so many gasoline refiners now use it instead.

Additionally, companies can get tax benefits for refining ethanol. Because large petroleum companies have done most of that refining to date, they have been the provision's main beneficiaries. In 2007, ethanol tax incentives caused the federal government to go without $3 billion it would otherwise have collected as tax revenues.

Currently, about 70 percent of the gasoline sold in the United States contains up to 10 percent ethanol. Ethanol manufacturers want to increase the amount to 15 percent for gasoline going into standard motor vehicles. Such a move would boost market demand for their product. If all regulatory approvals come through, such E15 gasoline could become common soon after 2010.

Ethanol additives offset the overall use of petroleum. However, ethanol has yet to take off as an alternative fuel in its own right. As of 2009 only about 2,000 of the nation's 160,000-plus fueling stations offered E85, a mixture of 85 percent ethanol and 15 percent gasoline.

Ethanol presents other issues. Farmers like the increased demand for their crops. However, the use of crops for ethanol can compete with other uses for those crops and with the growth of other crops. Greater demand for limited resources can push prices up.

For example, corn provides feed for livestock. Corn goes into a wide range of food products containing corn syrup. More obviously, people also consume corn in breads, cereals, vegetable dishes, and other foods.

The Congressional Budget Office found that federal ethanol fuel policies caused consumers to pay between 0.5 and 0.8 percent more for food. That was between 10 and 15 percent of the overall price increase for food of 5 percent from April 2007 to April 2008. As the report explained:

Producing ethanol for use in motor fuels increases the demand for corn, which ultimately raises the prices that consumers pay for a wide variety of foods at the grocery store, ranging from corn-syrup sweeteners found in soft drinks to meat, dairy and poultry products.

Food price increases also directly affect public welfare programs, such as the ones that provide school lunches and the Special Supplemental Nutrition Program for Women, Infants and Children. Other programs that are linked to a cost-of-living index would indirectly feel the effects.

The food versus fuel issue has drawn some harsh criticism. In 2007 Jean Ziegler, an expert for the United Nations on hunger issues, urged a five-year moratorium on biofuel production. With one in six people worldwide suffering from hunger, Ziegler felt that biofuel deprived people of their "right to food."

> [T]he effect of transforming hundreds and hundreds of thousands of tons of maize, of wheat, of beans, of palm oil into agricultural fuel is absolutely catastrophic for the hungry people. . . . It is a crime against humanity to convert agriculturally productive soil into soil which produces foodstuffs that will be burned [as] biofuel.

Afterward, the UN Food and Agriculture Organisation (FAO) said it regretted Ziegler's use of the phrase "crime against humanity." It also rejected his call for a temporary halt on ethanol production. As spokesperson Jeff Tschirley noted, "[A] moratorium that ignores the potential of biofuels to support rural development and assist the economies of developing countries would not, in our view, be a constructive approach to this topic."

John Mathews, a business professor at Australia's Macquarie University, has argued that food and biofuels production need not be "locked in conflict" in a "desperate zero-sum game." In other words, growth of one need not be at the expense of the other. He feels that restrictive aid-agency policies and other factors artificially limit farming productivity. Without such restrictions, he says, various countries could not only feed themselves but also export crops for biofuels and other uses. Their economies would grow, and the standard of living would rise.

When it comes to environmental benefits, ethanol's effects on greenhouse gases are debatable. Tailpipe emissions of cars running on ethanol are lower than those for cars running on gasoline. However, energy goes into growing the corn or other crop, refining the ethanol, and transporting it to users. Those all affect ethanol's net impact on the environment. Taking those factors into account, some critics feel ethanol isn't worth all the money, energy, and other resources that go into it.

Research by the Argonne National Laboratory suggests that ethanol's impact on greenhouse gas emissions depends largely on how producers make it. If a producer uses coal to generate the necessary power, switching to corn-based ethanol fuels could mean a 3 percent overall increase in greenhouse gas emissions, compared to gasoline. If that producer uses natural gas for power, though, corn ethanol would cut greenhouse gas emissions by about 30 percent.

Using other plant materials to make ethanol could cut greenhouse gas emissions more—by up to 50 percent, according to the Argonne National Laboratory researchers. Cellulosic ethanol is made from cellulose, the main component in plant cell walls.Possible sources include saw grass and wood chips. Instead of using crops with high sugar or starch content, cellulosic ethanol could come from woody, straw-like, or other plant parts with little commercial use right now. Making cellulosic ethanol would require less energy than making corn ethanol because of the different chemical reactions involved. Cellulosic ethanol would also reduce competition with food crops.

Compared to sugars or starches, cellulose is much more difficult to break down. Some pilot plants use enzymes, heat, or mechanical processes to help start the breakdown of cellulose. The process is more complex than the fermentation and distillation processes used for most commercially available ethanol. As of 2009 the United States had only a handful of pilot plants for making cellulosic ethanol. Large-scale production was at least five years away. Nor is it clear how the costs of producing cellulosic ethanol will ultimately compare with those for corn ethanol, other biofuels, or regular gasoline.

By 2030 biofuels and other organic fuels could replace almost one-third of current petroleum consumption in the United States, says a 2005 report by the Department of Energy and the Department of Agriculture. Getting to that point would require 1 billion dry tons of material to be converted into biofuels per year. That figure is about three-quarters of the total biofuel and other organic fuel potential of 1.3 billion dry tons, as estimated by the agencies. In other words, the one-third replacement goal is well within the country's reach.

Some scientists anticipate that a growing reliance on ethanol will almost certainly cause dramatic changes in land use. One group, including Jerry Melillo of the Marine Biological Laboratory in Woods Hole, has estimated that by 2050, biofuel crops could take up as much land as farms currently use for growing food.

"Many of the problems associated with biofuels are more generally problems with agriculture," Melillo said. Such problems include soil erosion and depletion and effects on biodiversity. Biofuel crops could also use up substantial amounts of water, energy, and other resources. "If it takes a lot of inputs and if negative environmental consequences persist," said Melillo, "then you clearly diminish the benefit you would derive from biofuels production."

In some areas, clearing land to grow biofuel crops can destroy forests and other wilderness areas. Primate scientist Jane Goodall and other conservation champions have warned against such habitat loss. Habitat loss is especially a concern in sensitive rain forest areas like Indonesia.

Clearing forest areas to plant biofuel crops could be counterproductive in other ways as well. Forests absorb large amounts of carbon dioxide from the air and hold the carbon within their plant structures. According to Holly Gibbs of Stanford University, tropical forests store as much carbon as fossil fuels would emit in the form of carbon dioxide over forty years of burning. If people clear forest areas to grow and harvest biofuel crops, those crops will absorb much less carbon dioxide than the forests that were there before. In Gibbs's view that would be like "burning rainforests in our gas tanks."

Researchers from Princeton University, Iowa State University, the Woods Hole Research Center, and Agricultural Conservation Economics (a consulting group in Maryland) set out to estimate such long-term effects on greenhouse gas emissions. They considered so-called indirect emissions from land cleared to raise more biofuel crops, plus land cleared to grow food in response to shortages caused by increased biofuel production. They calculated that cellulosic ethanol would cause a net increase in greenhouse gas emissions of about 50 percent over a thirty-year period. For corn-based ethanol the increase over thirty years would be nearly 100 percent. "Corn ethanol basically has no benefit, and it causes hunger," said Tim Searchinger, a Princeton researcher who worked on that 2008 report.

The state of California considered corn ethanol's impacts on land use when it issued low-carbon fuel emissions rules in 2009. The federal Environmental Protection Agency also took steps in 2009 to include land use effects in its calculations of ethanol's carbon dioxide emissions. The agency's proposal combined aspects of a half dozen models. However, scientific comments or eventual court challenges could change the agency's complicated formula.

Brazil and Biofuels

Brazil exports more biofuels than any other country, and it is second only to the United States in ethanol production. Brazil's biofuel industry relies mainly on sugarcane, which grows readily in the tropical South American country. The process of making ethanol from sugarcane is up to eight times more efficient than making it from corn. In other words, one unit of energy spent in growing and producing sugarcane ethanol will produce up to eight times as much energy as the same amount invested in making corn ethanol.

Brazil is also a world leader in biofuel usage. Gasoline sold in Brazil already contains at least 25 percent ethanol. Also, most new cars in Brazil can use either gasoline or pure ethanol. Brazil's light passenger vehicles now use more total ethanol than gasoline.

Brazilian President Luiz Inácio Lula da Silva has strongly supported the country's biofuels industry. Speaking at a 2008 conference, Lula explained:

Biofuels generate income and employment, especially in rural areas. They produce clean and renewable energy. They are an example of sustainability, of balance between environmental, social, and economic aspects. . . .

48

Brazil's production of ethanol from sugar cane occupies a tiny part of its agricultural land; it does not reduce the food production area; and it does not use that land for its production. Its expansion has been based on productivity gains and on better use of land for pasture. There is no risk of production in the Amazon region, nor of displacement of production. The same applies to biodiesel. . . .

Lula has also spoken out against protectionist measures and other pressures that would discourage biofuels produc-tion and exports.

At least through 2010, tariffs in the United States give domestic corn ethanol an edge over imported Brazilian ethanol made from sugarcane. However, recent Renewable Fuel Standards and other state actions with the United States could soon provide the market expansion that Brazil seeks.

"We know sugarcane ethanol has the lowest carbon emissions of any liquid biofuel produced today," said Joel Velasco, a spokesman for UNICA, the Brazilian sugarcane industry association. For Brazil, sugarcane ethanol is clearly a favorite fuel for alternative energy.

Fertilizers used to grow biofuel crops affect the atmosphere too. A 2009 study from the Paris-based International Council for Science found that modern farming practices would significantly increase emissions of nitrous oxide, another greenhouse gas. That finding is consistent with an earlier study by Paul Crutzen of Germany's Max Planck Institute and other scientists in Europe and the United States. Nitrous oxide stays in the atmosphere longer and affects global climate more than carbon dioxide does.

The studies determined that nitrous oxide emissions could negate any purported climate-change benefits from using biofuels instead of fossil fuels. Robert Howarth of Cornell University, who cochaired the 2009 study project, summed up his group's conclusion:

> The policy of using ethanol to reduce reliance on the fossil fuels that cause global warming is self-defeating because ethanol production actually increases net greenhouse gas emissions.

Despite such concerns, ethanol will likely make up a growing percentage of transportation fuel used in the United States. Many companies have a significant economic stake in seeing ethanol succeed, including farmers and fuel refiners. Ethanol's ability to reduce reliance on foreign oil also plays a big part in the political support it commands.

Biodiesel—French-Fried Fuel?

Sometimes singer Willie Nelson's Mercedes smells like french fries. At other times it has a definite peanut odor. It all depends on what type of waste oil Nelson used to make his biodiesel fuel. Nelson's BioWillie fuel blends 20 percent biodiesel from plant oils with 80 percent petroleum diesel. While the brand won't become a top seller soon, at least a dozen commercial stations have sold it.

Willie Nelson holds up the nozzle before filling his bus with BioWillie Diesel Fuel at an alternative fuel station in San Diego, California.

Biodiesel is an alternative fuel made from plant or animal oils. Compared to petroleum diesel fuel, it burns cleaner and is biodegradable. Like ethanol, biodiesel comes from renewable sources and would reduce reliance on foreign oil imports. Unlike ethanol, biodiesel is also easier to sell through existing fuel stations and supply networks. Early trials have already sent biodiesel through existing pipelines. Unlike ethanol, it is much less likely to increase in water content and degrade significantly while traveling through a pipeline.

Since 2001 more than 600 retail outlets have sold fuels containing biodiesel. A 20-percent/80-percent blend with petroleum diesel is most common. However, many diesel engines can run well on fuel with varying percentages of biodiesel—even up to 100 percent.

Globally, rapeseed (canola) is the most common oil used in biodiesel, accounting for roughly five-sixths of production as of 2006. Other feedstocks, or raw materials, are sunflower oil, soybean oil, and palm oil. Even algae is a potential source of raw materials for biodiesel. Some colleges have even started recycling their waste cooking oil to make biodiesel, including Keene State College in New Hampshire and Sinclair Community College in Ohio.

Vegetable oil can't go straight from the fryer into the fuel tank. Generally, processing involves a chemical reaction with the oil and some form of alcohol in the presence of a catalyst. (A catalyst affects the speed of a chemical reaction but is not actually part of it.) About 10 percent winds up as a thick, oily by-product called glycerin, along with some other chemicals. The rest is fuel-quality biodiesel.

Biodiesel does have some drawbacks. For example, it can thicken at very low temperatures, which might affect its combustion. More important, waste oil alone probably could not supply enough biodiesel to meet the majority of America's transportation fuel needs. According to chemical engineer Joseph Shuster, using all the soybean oil currently produced would replace barely 7 percent of the nation's current diesel fuel use.

Plant-oil production could expand, of course. Indeed, one acre of sunflowers can produce between 63 and 100 gallons of biodiesel. However, the expansion of cropland causes concerns similar to those some scientists have voiced about ethanol.

Like ethanol, biodiesel may become a larger component of diesel fuel. Since 2005, for example, Minnesota has required that all diesel fuel sold there contain at least 2 percent biodiesel. The relative price of petroleum diesel fuel versus biodiesel fuel, as well as other factors, will affect the future demand for biodiesel. Meanwhile, research and promotion of biodiesel as an alternative fuel will continue.

Biomass Electricity

Parts of the United States are now generating electricity from biomass, or waste organic matter. In some cases power suppliers can burn plant waste directly. For example, burning wood or other plant material can heat water to generate steam the way burning coal or fossil fuels would. In cofiring, the biomass is mixed with some other fuel, such as coal. For both direct burning and cofiring, the biomass fuels are renewable and generally do not involve foreign imports. However, they still present significant challenges for pollution control. Energy conversion efficiencies are about 20 percent for direct firing and 33 percent or slightly more for cofiring.

Pollution problems are fewer if power suppliers first convert biomass into a gaseous fuel known as synthetic gas, or syngas. The most efficient gasification can also boost the energy conversion efficiency of biomass fuel to roughly 60 percent. Gasification techniques vary, depending on the type of waste material. For example, dried wood or other plant material may go into a high-temperature, high-pressure reactor with steam. Manure and some other kinds of farm waste typically go into a digester machine. Chemicals or bacteria break down complex molecules in the waste to produce methane gas. For other waste, such as landfill gas, the material may already be in the form of methane.

About 60 percent of biomass electricity comes from wood-based materials. Examples include wood chips and forestry residue from logging, sawmills, and pulp operations. The rest comes from farm waste, municipal waste, and landfill gas.

Biomass's big attraction is that it uses materials that would otherwise require disposal as waste. Towns and businesses produce lots of waste. Commercial farms also produce mounds of plant debris and animal manure. Already, the United States has approximately 125 manure digesters working to produce biogas from animal waste.

Biomass is also renewable. For example, tree-logging operations plant new trees to replace the ones they cut down. Environmental benefits also include lower greenhouse gas emissions when biomass replaces coal in electricity generation. If energy producers convert biomass to syngas before burning, pollutant levels can be even lower than those from natural gas because the conversion process traps heavy metals and some other pollutants that would otherwise have gone into the air.

Generating energy from biomass does have some drawbacks. Transporting feedstocks, such as farm wastes, uses energy, which produces its own pollution and greenhouse gas emissions. Building syngas production facilities and electric power plants close to feedstock sources reduces that problem.

Financial obstacles factor in as well. To date, syngas has commanded fairly low prices in the energy market. Suppliers have faced resistance from utility companies about connecting to the electricity grid. Also, in the case of farm waste, processors must still dispose of waste residues after the feedstock goes through a biodigester. Cooperative ventures among farms can reduce some of these problems, but they won't eliminate the issues.

Biomass's small share of the energy market will likely increase as technologies for utilizing it advance. Alternative energy champions would argue that every bit of sustainable energy that doesn't rely on imports helps.

4 Can Hydrogen Help?

WHO WOULDN'T WANT A FUEL THAT LEFT ONLY clean water as a waste product? And wouldn't it be great if that fuel was one of Earth's most common elements? In his 2003 State of the Union address, President George W. Bush sought $1.2 billion in research funding for hydrogen-powered automobiles. In a follow-up speech Bush declared, "Hydrogen fuel cells represent one of the most encouraging, innovative technologies of our era."

Before the year ended, Toyota Motor Corporation unveiled an experimental hydrogen-powered car. Models from Honda and General Motors soon followed. So far, though, no hydrogen cars are on the market for purchase by ordinary consumers.

Nor is America anywhere close to having the hydrogen economy that Bush and his supporters forecast. Some of the reasons relate mainly to the ways hydrogen energy is produced, stored, and delivered. Environmental concerns and costs have also hindered the development of hydrogen energy.

Hydrogen as Fuel—Power to Go?

The good news is that hydrogen exists almost everywhere on planet Earth. The bad news is that it's almost always bound to some other element. Processing must first separate hydrogen from any other elements with which it is chemically bound.

Hydrogen isn't used as a fuel in the same way that gasoline, diesel, or biofuels are. Hydrogen fuel must be oxidized, or bonded

A man fills up his hydrogen fuel cell car at the first commercial hydrogen dispenser in the United States.

to oxygen, without flames. Otherwise, disaster can occur. One of the most notorious accidents occurred in 1937, when the *Hindenburg* airship, which was filled with hydrogen, caught fire and killed three dozen people.

Oxidizing hydrogen in a controlled way requires a fuel cell. A hydrogen fuel cell is like a battery, with terminals called an anode and a cathode. At the anode the hydrogen gas ionizes. In other words it separates into positively charged protons and negatively charged electrons. The protons pass through a membrane to the cathode. The cathode attracts the electrons, but they can't go through the membrane. Instead, the electrons travel to the cathode through wires that form an electric circuit. The electric circuit provides electricity to power a car or other device.

Meanwhile, oxygen from the air ionizes at the cathode. When the hydrogen's protons and electrons meet up with those from the oxygen, a chemical reaction takes place. The resulting water and heat become the system's waste products. Conventional batteries die when they use up their stored chemical fuel. A hydrogen fuel cell can keep going as long as it gets hydrogen and oxygen.

So far, hydrogen fuel cells have been very expensive. The proton exchange membranes, or PEMs, cost about $500 per square meter as of 2008. Moreover, most PEMs so far have needed platinum in order to work. Platinum is both expensive and rare.

As a result, price tags for hydrogen-powered cars probably won't come close to those of existing conventional or hybrid vehicles for decades. When Honda's FCX Clarity came out in 2008, its production cost was hundreds of thousands of dollars per car. In contrast, hybrid cars are already available at costs close to those for cars with conventional gasoline engines.

Separating hydrogen from various compounds also requires energy, which adds to the fuel's cost. Natural gas is currently the main source of hydrogen fuel, and natural gas is a fossil fuel. Extracting hydrogen from natural gas produces carbon dioxide and other wastes. That's bad news for people who care about greenhouse gas emissions and climate change.

Researchers at the Massachusetts Institute of Technology (MIT) and Cambridge University have concluded that net greenhouse gas emissions from hydrogen cars would be no better than those from diesel-powered hybrid cars. "Ignoring the emissions and energy use involved in making and delivering the [hydrogen] fuel and manufacturing the vehicle gives a misleading impression," said MIT researcher Malcolm Weiss.

Electrolysis could be a cleaner way to make hydrogen. The process separates water into hydrogen and oxygen—which is basically the reverse of what the hydrogen fuel cell does. However, most techniques for performing electrolysis are energy intensive. If that energy comes from coal or other fossil fuels, climate-change concerns will remain.

Nuclear power plants might improve the efficiency of electrolysis by providing high-temperature steam from their operations. Making enough fuel for the hydrogen-powered equivalent of today's cars would require roughly two thousand newer-style pebble bed reactors. As of 2007 the United States didn't yet have any pebble bed reactors working.

Getting mass-produced hydrogen to fuel cell users is another challenge. Hydrogen gas is highly flammable, so special safeguards are necessary. The fuel could not travel in pipelines presently used for distributing petroleum products. Fearful communities may object to having any separate pipeline system built nearby.

Trucks and railcars are possible delivery vehicles. However, it would take energy to pressurize and refrigerate the hydrogen so it could be shipped as a liquid. Trucks and railcars would also use energy—most likely from fossil fuels—to get the hydrogen from one place to another. That would boost costs and detract from any environmental benefits.

Hydrogen fueling stations could potentially perform electrolysis on site. However, that would boost the costs for building and maintaining such stations. More than five dozen hydrogen fueling stations have already opened across the country, about half of them in California. However, consumers could buy hydrogen at only six of that state's twenty-six stations as of 2009. The California Fuel Cell Partnership has announced plans to build at least forty-six retail hydrogen fuel stations by 2014. Far more would be needed before fuel cells could play a major part in U.S. transportation.

Researchers will continue to search for better ways to handle, store, and deliver hydrogen for fuel cells. For example, some researchers are studying how polymer foams might help with the process.

Another way to solve the transportation and delivery problems would be for end users to have their own, small hydrogen-extraction devices. Consumers might fill their cars' hydrogen tanks from a refrigerator-sized hydrogen extractor at their home, for example. Household electricity (most likely generated by fossil fuels) would power the device.

One concept comes from a British company, ITM Power. The company is developing a refrigerator-sized electrolysis device. ITM's device would use a different type of membrane to separate the hydrogen and oxygen gas after they're separated from water. The novel membrane could also make fuel cells cheaper, the company has said. Instead of the platinum needed for PEMs, fuel cells with the company's technology could use nickel, which is far cheaper. The product is not yet in mass production. Nor is it clear whether it would be able to produce enough electricity for the average car driver's needs.

Another process, proposed by Jerry Woodall at Purdue University, would use an alloy of aluminum and gallium to produce hydrogen fuel. When the metal pellets come in contact with water, they react to produce hydrogen and aluminum oxide. The gallium from the alloy doesn't get used up and can be recycled. "The

How a Fuel Cell Makes Electricity from Hydrogen Fuel

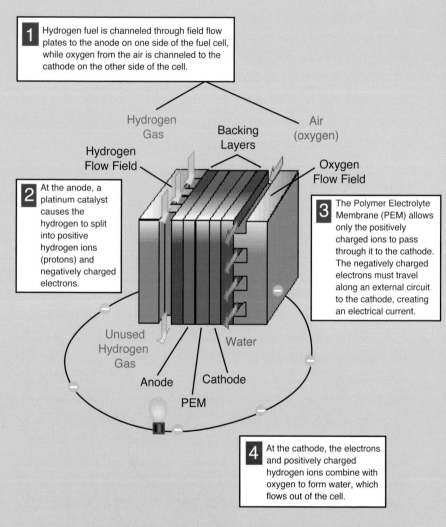

1 Hydrogen fuel is channeled through field flow plates to the anode on one side of the fuel cell, while oxygen from the air is channeled to the cathode on the other side of the cell.

Hydrogen Gas

Backing Layers

Air (oxygen)

Hydrogen Flow Field

Oxygen Flow Field

2 At the anode, a platinum catalyst causes the hydrogen to split into positive hydrogen ions (protons) and negatively charged electrons.

3 The Polymer Electrolyte Membrane (PEM) allows only the positively charged ions to pass through it to the cathode. The negatively charged electrons must travel along an external circuit to the cathode, creating an electrical current.

Unused Hydrogen Gas

Water

Anode

Cathode

PEM

4 At the cathode, the electrons and positively charged hydrogen ions combine with oxygen to form water, which flows out of the cell.

Source: United States Department of Energy, "How They Work: PEM Fuel Cells," undated, http://www.fueleconomy.gov/feg/fcv_pem.shtml (accessed August 24, 2009).

hydrogen is generated on demand, so you only produce as much as you need when you need it," said Woodall. Cutting the costs of recycling the aluminum oxide by-product would be a big step toward making the process economical on a large scale.

Unlike petroleum, hydrogen power wouldn't involve huge imports from overseas. If the technical difficulties can be dealt with, hydrogen power could someday play a significant part in the United States' energy mix. However, that day won't come in the next ten or twenty years. Indeed, it could be much farther off.

Critics of hydrogen energy, such as Joseph Romm of the Center for American Progress, doubt whether the hydrogen economy will ever be more than just hype. In addition to all its other problems, Romm says the technology faces a huge "chicken-and-egg problem." Companies won't make significant numbers of hydrogen-powered cars until they can sell them at a profit. Consumers won't buy many of those expensive cars until they're sure they can get fuel easily. That fuel won't be readily available until there's either an infrastructure to deliver it or facilities to generate it on-site. And companies won't build an extensive delivery system or mass-produce on-site hydrogen generators until a ready market exists.

Romm and other critics contend that efforts spent on developing hydrogen energy draw attention and resources away from other technologies. In their view, talk about hydrogen energy makes people think that the country is making progress toward developing alternative energy sources. Meanwhile, present policies and technology encourage more fossil fuel use.

In short, critics say, the hydrogen economy is no cure-all for America's energy problems. Nor does it promise to play any significant role in energy generation soon. Supporters respond that switching to any new energy source takes time. They expect future generations could benefit greatly from current work on hydrogen energy.

Iceland's Hydrogen Experiment

Could Iceland's cars and buses run on hydrogen by 2040? "It is possible with the technology that is available today," says Maria Maack, environmental manager at Icelandic New Energy. Whether people commit the resources and organize everything to do that is another story.

Icelandic New Energy was founded after utilities, research institutions, carmaker Daimler AG, and global energy company Shell decided to work together in trying to develop a hydrogen economy to power the island nation's transportation system. Iceland already uses lots of geothermal and hydroelectric power to generate electricity and heat buildings. Now the company feels it can free Iceland from its reliance on imported oil for transportation.

By 2003 Shell had the world's first retail hydrogen fuel pump installed near its regular pumps at a Grjótháls gasoline station. The first hydrogen customers were three fuel-cell buses. Customers with passenger cars can also use the pump, including those with specially designed Daimler A-Class electric cars and modified Toyota Priuses.

As of 2009, fewer than two dozen vehicles were using the station's hydrogen pumps. The hydrogen bus program ended due to lack of profitability. Inconveniently, the buses had also required two thirty-minute fill-ups per day. Meanwhile, a second filling station had opened at Ægisgarður, mainly to service the *Elding*, a whale-watching ship.

Skeptics have suggested that Iceland promote electric cars instead. Maack agrees that electric cars may eventually gain up to one-third of the car market. However, electric cars cannot travel far before they require refueling. Hydrogen cars or hybrid hydrogen-electric vehicles would provide greater range and convenience. Hydrogen would also help the country's fishing industry, whose vessels often travel greater distances than electric batteries can reliably provide without recharging.

Cost is another issue. Hydrogen cars' price tags are currently several times higher than those for conventional luxury cars. Even if they could afford them, the country's residents wouldn't be able to buy hydrogen-powered cars on the mass market until 2015 or 2020. Before then, much more investment in basic infrastructure is needed: facilities to produce hydrogen, a broader distribution system, and so on. "It is a question of financing," says Maack.

Much also depends on the relative cost of new fuels compared to those for fossil fuels. Costs for hydrogen and other forms of alternative energy are high, because they reflect most of the technology's start-up costs. In contrast, fossil fuel prices have so far failed to reflect the true costs of the fuel's carbon dioxide and other emissions.

"The virtues of clean technology cost, but polluting does not cost," observes Maack. "So either humanity puts a price tag on pollution, or nothing happens."

5 Nuclear? Unclear

"AS A ZERO-CARBON ENERGY SOURCE, NUCLEAR power must be part of our energy mix as we work towards energy independence and meeting the challenge of global warming," announced Steven Chu, the Nobel Prize–winning physicist who became Secretary of Energy in 2009. Nuclear power has been part of the U.S. energy mix since the 1950s. As of 2009 the industry's 104 reactors in 31 states supplied about one-fifth of the United States' electricity needs. At the same time the Nuclear Regulatory Commission needed to act on applications for approximately one hundred new or expanded facilities.

Supporters say that nuclear energy can provide plentiful and reliable energy without contributing to climate change. Fission of a single gram of uranium can produce as much energy as burning 525 gallons of gasoline. Unlike gasoline, uranium fission does not emit greenhouse gases or other air pollutants. It also would not have to come from foreign countries that have tense relationships with the United States.

However, nuclear fuel and its waste products are radioactive. Because of this, opponents argue that nuclear power presents unacceptable safety risks, environmental dilemmas, and security worries. Finding acceptable sites for building reactors and waste storage facilities, as well as arranging for financing, are also significant problems.

Nuclear lab technicians wear protective suits while testing radiation levels.

The ABCs of Nuclear Fission

All current and planned nuclear power plants use nuclear fission to generate power. Fission involves splitting an atom's nucleus into smaller parts. Nuclear fission is fundamentally different from conventional burning of fuel, which combines oxygen with other compounds so that new chemical bonds form. Nuclear fission actually changes matter into energy. The process is an application of Einstein's famous equation, $E=mc^2$, which means that energy equals mass times the speed of light, squared. Even a tiny bit of mass can release huge quantities of energy.

In a typical pressurized water reactor, uranium serves as the fuel. Just as you use a cue stick to shoot one ball into a triangle of pool balls and start a game, a device shoots neutrons into fuel-grade uranium to trigger the fission reaction. Atoms that started out as uranium-235, a particular form of uranium, break apart into barium and krypton. The process gives off some extra neutrons and other atomic particles.

The extra neutrons can then strike other uranium atoms, causing the process to repeat in a chain reaction. After each uranium-235 atom splits, the mass of the barium and krypton atoms, plus other particles, is just a bit less than that of the split uranium atom. That tiny bit of matter becomes energy.

Nuclear fission produces about a million times more energy than would result from burning a comparable mass of fossil fuels. "And nuclear fission is converting less than one percent of the available mass," notes Tony Rothman, a physics professor at Princeton University.

Nuclear reactors can use other types of fuel, including plutonium and another type of uranium. After the fission of these other fuels, different products remain. However, the result is basically the same: The nuclear reaction produces fundamentally different elements, and it converts some of the fuel's mass into a tremendous amount of energy. Nuclear power plants take advantage of that energy to heat water and produce steam, which runs electric turbines. For safety and efficiency reasons, though, nuclear plants must carefully control the fission reactions.

If spare neutrons zip away before they can get into another uranium atom's nucleus, the chain reaction will stop. Think about how, in golf, controlled putting is more likely to sink a ball on the green than is whacking it with all your strength. At the same time, it shouldn't be too easy for the neutrons to split apart more atoms. An out-of-control fission reaction is like a bomb—too much energy is released at one time. And if the reactor gets too hot, it could have a meltdown or other accident. If such an accident exposes the nuclear fuel, it can release potentially dangerous radiation.

In short, a nuclear reactor has to run "just right." To keep a reactor running properly, engineers space rod-shaped pieces of nuclear fuel at optimal distances within a reactor's core. Water (or sometimes another material) surrounds the fuel rods and acts as a moderator. The moderator slows down the spare neutrons that result from the fission reaction. This increases the neutrons' likelihood of splitting uranium atoms' nuclei within various fuel rods.

While the moderator helps to keep the chain reaction going, control rods can slow or stop it. Material in the rods, such as boron or cadmium, absorbs the neutrons that strike them. Once that happens, the neutrons can't trigger any more fission. Control rods adjust to different heights, so power plants can regulate what fraction of the fuel rods takes part in the fission reactions. If the rods are down all the way, the whole reactor shuts down.

Engineers design control rod systems so they will drop into place automatically if a potentially dangerous situation occurs. Otherwise, positioning the control rods helps engineers use the uranium or other nuclear fuel efficiently. Systems also allow engineers to make small adjustments to meet changes in energy demand or deal with other factors.

Cooling is a crucial factor in nuclear plant design because

heat buildup can be dangerous. As neutrons travel through the moderator material, they transfer heat to it. The water thus acts as a coolant for the system.

There are several types of nuclear reactors, but they all work in similar ways. In a pressurized-water reactor, heat-exchange piping transfers heat from the moderator water to other purified water, which turns to steam. The arrangement draws off heat from the primary coolant—the moderator water—without transferring low-level radioactivity from that water. The steam then powers electric generators.

Another system of pipes transfers excess heat from the steam to other water that usually comes from a nearby river or lake. The purified water can then run through the system again. Meanwhile, large towers cool down the lake or river water to near-air temperatures. That water can then return to the river or lake.

Other types of nuclear reactors do pretty much the same thing, but with some variations. Heavy-water reactors use water whose hydrogen atoms have one proton plus one neutron as a moderator/primary coolant. Because heavy water absorbs fewer neutrons than regular water, such reactors can operate more efficiently. The efficiency benefits can save fuel or let reactors use uranium that has not been enriched. (Enriched fuel has gone through processing to increase the concentration of fissionable uranium.)

Breeder reactors use mixtures of uranium, plutonium, and sometimes thorium. Neutrons from some of the fission reactions inside the reactor convert nonfissionable uranium-238 into fissionable plutonium-239. Because the reactor makes and uses more fissionable nuclear fuel than it starts out with, engineers use the term "breeder."

Scary Situations

Fears about nuclear power made front-page news in 1979, when an accident shut down the Three Mile Island power plant in

Middletown, Pennsylvania. In the country's most significant nuclear accident, as much as 13 million curies of radioactivity escaped into the surrounding air. (A curie is a measure of radioactivity.) For more than three decades after the accident, power companies did not build any new nuclear power plants in the United States. Existing facilities continued to run without major incidents.

An investigation revealed that an alarm sounded for Three Mile Island's new Number 2 reactor in the early morning hours of March 28, 1979. One pump malfunction triggered another, causing the plant's giant generator to shut down. Within seconds, control rods stopped nuclear fission within the reactor's core. The system then blew off a burst of superheated, radioactive water from within the reactor. After discharging the water, a pressure-release valve stayed open, letting too much steam escape. Other valves that should have let in new coolant water incorrectly stayed shut. Without more water to carry away excess heat, the reactor's core temperature climbed. The excessive heat damaged the fuel rods and allowed radioactive cooling water to leak out of the reactor. What should have been a minor incident quickly became an official "general emergency."

Fortunately, no one died as the result of the accident. Although Governor Richard Thornburgh recommended that pregnant women and children stay at least five miles away from the facility, the government stopped short of calling for a general evacuation. Nonetheless, public fears ran high.

Further fuel for those fears came from *The China Syndrome*. That Hollywood blockbuster about a possible nuclear meltdown opened in theaters just twelve days before the Three Mile Island accident occurred. People worried that the worst-case scenario described in that movie could have happened at Three Mile Island. In an attempt to prevent public panic, President Jimmy Carter visited Three Mile Island on April 1, 1979. By that time, though, nuclear power's reputation with the public had suffered.

Seven years later the world learned about another nuclear power plant accident. On April 26, 1986, the Number 4 reactor exploded at the Chernobyl Nuclear Power Plant in Ukraine. Although the Soviet Union tried to hush up the accident, news—and tremendous amounts of radiation—spread. Later reports linked the deaths of fifty-six people, including nine children, directly to the accident. Among the 600,000 people who suffered the most radiation exposure, another 4,000 may have died prematurely from cancer.

The Chernobyl reactor used graphite instead of water to promote the chain reaction. Graphite is more likely to lead to overheating than is water. The United States does not have any power plants designed like the Chernobyl reactor that failed. Nonetheless, the disaster damaged nuclear power's reputation even more.

Safety continues to be a concern. Strict laws and regulations are already on the books. However, critics such as the Union of Concerned Scientists (UCS) argue that the Nuclear Regulatory Commission's enforcement of these safety regulations has been uneven. The incident at Three Mile Island showed that minor incidents could quickly grow into major problems. The more that can be done to prevent human and mechanical errors, the better.

Security Worries

Deliberate attacks on nuclear power plants could be more devastating than any previous terrorist strikes. The government beefed up security at nuclear power plants and other facilities after the 9/11 terrorist attacks in 2001. However, UCS and other critics claim that nuclear power plants remain too vulnerable to sabotage.

Worries about sabotage surfaced when the federal government accidentally posted a list of nuclear facilities on the Internet in 2009. The government said the list did not contain classified information, but Department of Energy secretary Steven Chu admitted the incident was "a little embarrassing." "We don't want to make this easier for people to get this kind of information,"

A militia member guards a "forbidden area" after the accident at Chernobyl.

added Thomas D'Agostino, head of the National Nuclear Security Administration.

The nature of nuclear fuel raises more concerns. Nuclear power plants in the United States have generally used only low-enriched uranium. About 3 percent of typical uranium fuel is fissionable uranium-235, which has 92 protons and 143 neutrons in its nucleus. Neutrons can split those atoms apart in the fission chain reaction. Most of the rest of the fuel is nonfissionable uranium. The makeup of low-enriched uranium prevents possible terrorists from using the fuel to make weapons. Also, because uranium-235 makes up only about one percent of all naturally occurring uranium, the supply of nuclear fuel is limited. In other words, nuclear power is not renewable. At some point, fuel will run out.

Nuclear power plants would have fewer worries about fuel supplies if they could get other forms of uranium to undergo fission. Breeder reactors can do this. During the fission reaction, they convert uranium-238 to fissionable plutonium-239. The process produces more usable fuel for fission.

Breeder reactors generally use some plutonium in their starting fuel mix. The easiest way for breeder reactors to get plutonium is through reprocessing spent nuclear fuel from uranium-235 plants. However, that task poses significant safety risks and creates more nuclear waste.

Plutonium can also be used in nuclear weapons. Detecting a theft of fissionable plutonium could be difficult. Critics worry that a nuclear attack using stolen fuel could occur before officials even learned that the fuel was missing.

What About the Waste?

Spent nuclear waste can't just go in the trash. Its radioactivity poses serious risks. People who are exposed to unsafe levels can suffer fatal radiation sickness. Exposure to excess radiation over time also causes various types of cancer. Any disposal method should obviously protect people from unsafe exposure. The method should also ensure that radioactive materials don't contaminate soil, groundwater, or air.

Spent nuclear fuel is not only radioactive, it will stay that way for thousands of years. A radioactive material's half-life is the time required for half of its mass to decay. In radioactive materials, to decay means to shed enough particles so that an atom becomes a different element. The half-life of uranium-235 is 704 million years. The half-life of uranium-238, the form that makes up most of naturally occurring uranium and uranium fuel rods, is 4.46 billion years. Although the proportion that stays radioactive grows smaller with each half-life, radioactivity will stay above levels of concern for many half-lives.

As this century opened, the United States already had more than 200,000 tons of nuclear waste waiting for disposal. Each year the average nuclear reactor adds another 20 to 30 tons. As this book goes to press, the United States does not yet have any approved long-term disposal solution for its nuclear waste.

Nevada's Yucca Mountain repository project had been the only disposal site under serious consideration by the U.S. government for more than twenty years. The government has already spent

This caution sign at the Hanford nuclear site in Washington State warns against entering this "burial ground" for radioactive waste, much of which came from plutonium production.

more than $10 billion and several decades studying its geology and suitability. Before the site received approval, the Nuclear Regulatory Commission was to complete additional studies at an estimated cost of $40 million.

In 2009, however, it appeared that the Yucca Mountain waste site might never open after all. Energy Secretary Steven Chu told a Senate committee that the United States should find some other solution for long-term nuclear waste disposal. "I think we can do a better job," Chu said.

Meanwhile, spent nuclear fuel remains in temporary storage at the country's 104 nuclear power plants. The Nuclear Energy Institute, an industry group, feels that there is no rush to find a final dump site. In its view the temporary storage areas are safe "indefinitely." Eventually, though, the United States will have to do something about its nuclear waste. Until then, critics worry about expanding nuclear power's share of the U.S. energy mix.

Dollars and Sense

From a financial standpoint, critics question whether the United States can afford nuclear energy. Building any new nuclear energy plant is a major financial undertaking. Other technologies can help deal with peak energy demands or allow gradual shifts from one form of energy to another. Other technologies can also start on a small scale and expand as their markets grow. Nuclear power plants can't.

"They only come in one size: extra large," former vice president Al Gore told a Senate committee. Yet capital budgets face limits, and energy demands fluctuate. As Gore sees it, "Utility executives become allergic to placing large bets . . . with uncertain construction costs over a long period of time into the future." Meanwhile, though, the Energy Information Administration anticipates that tax credits and other government policies will help increase the nation's nuclear power capacity.

The Nuclear Energy Institute maintains that nuclear plants are "the lowest-cost producer of baseload electricity"—electricity that is on and available all the time. However, it's unclear whether that assertion accounts for all construction costs. New facilities would have to build those costs and a rate of return for investors into their rates for the useful life of the plant. Political and regulatory issues add significant expenses too.

Taking all costs into account, electricity from a new nuclear power plant could cost customers $14 to $30 more per megawatt-hour than electricity from a coal-fired power plant. Anticipated rules that put a price on carbon dioxide emissions will likely shrink the cost gap between nuclear energy and electricity generated from fossil fuels. Critics concede that point, but they argue that the country would be better served by other alternative energy technologies—ones that don't pose the risks related to radioactive fuel and wastes.

Nuclear energy advocates feel that the country can't afford not to expand its nuclear power capacity. In their view nuclear power is the most reliable option for meeting baseload power. Most other low-carbon-emission electricity technologies have built-in variability factors, capacity limits, geography factors, or large land area requirements.

Nuclear energy advocates also note that between now and 2030, the United States faces an anticipated 21 percent growth in its annual energy demands. They feel that the only technology that can reliably supply enough electricity to meet the country's growing energy needs in the twenty-first century is nuclear.

Is Fusion in Our Future?

Fusion is the joining of two or more atoms to form new elements. Fusion occurs naturally in the Sun and other stars. Whether it can ever provide significant amounts of reliable electric power on Earth is highly doubtful.

Within the Sun's core a chain reaction starts when hydrogen nuclei join together. The end result is helium and leftover atomic particles. The mass of those end products is just a bit less than that of the original hydrogen nuclei. The remaining matter gets converted to energy. Einstein's equation, $E=mc^2$, still applies.

Energy from nuclear fusion heats the Sun's core to more than 15 million °C. As stars exhaust their supply of hydrogen, heavier elements begin to fuse. The hydrogen fuel in the Sun will last for approximately 5 billion years.

Fusion sounds as if it could be the ultimate alternative energy solution. Earth's atmosphere has lots of hydrogen, so the fuel supply wouldn't be a problem. The by-product of hydrogen fusion, helium, is a fairly safe, inert gas. Radioactivity is not an issue with fusion. Nor would fusion aggravate global climate change. Moreover, the energy yield would be enormous.

However, fusion requires incredibly high temperatures—millions of degrees. Reaching and maintaining such temperatures would require putting lots of energy into the system. The immense heat would also melt any material container.

Small-scale experiments have achieved fusion by isolating the raw materials in special magnetic fields. So far, those experiments have used more energy to generate the magnetic fields than the fusion process produced.

Now the International Thermonuclear Experimental Reactor (ITER) project is working on a doughnut-shaped apparatus, called a tokamak, which will create huge magnetic fields. If all goes well, ITER will sustain fusion for about five minutes at a time and produce ten times more energy than goes into the process. However, the $15 billion, internationally supported research project in southern France won't get to that point until 2018.

Even if the ITER project succeeds, it would take decades and billions more dollars before the world had anything close to a practical tokamak fusion reactor. It's also unclear how expensive

Nuclear Power
in India

India is turning to nuclear power to meet its expanding energy needs. Within five years India aims to generate 22,000 megawatts (MW) of nuclear power annually. That's roughly a fivefold increase over 2008 levels of 4,120 MW.

Reaching that point will be a challenge. On average, India's existing nuclear power plants ran at half capacity in 2008. For more than thirty years the United States and other countries had refused to cooperate with India in the nuclear energy market because India had refused to sign the 1968 Nuclear Non-Proliferation Treaty. India also acted against the spirit of that treaty by testing an atomic weapon in 1974.

A 2008 treaty cleared the way for India to obtain nuclear fuel in the international market, but only for civilian purposes. That treaty is informally called a "123 Agreement," because section 123 of the Atomic Energy Act of 1954 requires such treaties before the United States can cooperate with other countries on nuclear power. The 2008 treaty also opened the way for American and European companies to work on new nuclear reactors for India. Companies could get billions of dollars' worth of contract awards for building up to twenty new nuclear plants.

If India meets its targets for expanding nuclear power, "We will be meeting 20 to 25 percent of the country's total electricity needs," said S. K. Jain, chairman of the government-owned Nuclear Power Corporation of India. India has huge energy needs. As 2009 began, almost 400 million people still lacked regular access to electricity.

power generated by such a reactor would be or what safety issues might exist.

To get around the problem of high temperatures, some scientists have tried to achieve cold fusion. In other words, they want to achieve fusion at room temperature. The concept of cold fusion made global headlines in 1989. Researchers Stanley Pons of the University of Utah and Martin Fleischmann of Southampton University told the press they had successfully done cold fusion experiments. Other scientists could not duplicate the results, though.

Also, Pons and Fleischmann skipped over the standard peer-review process that would have taken place if they had first published their results in a scientific journal. That process would have noted shortcomings in their work. Fallout from these announcements discredited Pons and Fleischmann in scientific circles. In the public's eye the promise of cold fusion energy was just a hoax.

Despite the Pons and Fleischmann fiasco some scientists have continued to pursue the possibility of fusion at low temperatures. To avoid association with Pons and Fleischmann, researchers now avoid using the term "cold fusion." Instead, researchers use the term "low-energy nuclear reaction," or LENR.

Some of the more promising work with LENR involves injecting deuterium (a hydrogen atom with one proton and one neutron) into molecules containing the metal palladium. Basically, the experiments aim to get deuterium atoms to join together slowly within the metal's latticelike structure. Some researchers have claimed that their experiments produced more energy than they used to operate the process.

In 2009, for example, Navy researcher Pamela Mosier-Boss reported on her group's work at an American Chemical Society conference in Utah. The group ran a current through a solution of palladium chloride and so-called heavy water, water containing deuterium. They detected "highly energetic neutrons," which they saw as evidence that nuclear fusion could be occurring within the experimental device. "Our finding is very significant," Mosier-Boss said.

Some people hope that LENR could lead to the production of cheap, practical energy. Others remain skeptical about the Navy group's work. "It fails to provide a theoretical rationale to explain how fusion could occur at room temperatures," Rice University physicist Paul Padley told the *Houston Chronicle*. "And in its analysis, the research paper fails to exclude other sources for the production of neutrons."

As with other issues, scientists generally resist accepting a study's conclusions unless and until other researchers can reliably duplicate results each time an experiment is performed. So far, this hasn't happened with LENR.

LENR research will likely continue. For the foreseeable future, however, fusion is not a viable option for alternative energy.

6 Solar Energy: Harnessing the Sun's Power

THE SUN PROVIDES LIGHT AND WARMS THE PLANET to temperatures that support life. It supplies energy to grow food. It drives global weather patterns. Why not harness some of the Sun's power to deal with the world's energy issues?

Many people see solar energy as the ultimate alternative energy choice. Representatives of the photovoltaic industry, which manufactures solar panels and solar cells, have announced a goal of generating at least 10 percent of the United States' domestic electricity by 2030. Solar energy has a long way to go if it's going to meet that goal. In 2009 solar energy produced less than one percent of the nation's electricity.

Solar energy offers lots of promise. Like other alternative energy options, however, solar power is not a magical cure-all for the United States' energy problems. This chapter looks at ways that solar power can generate electricity, what it would take to expand solar energy, and other challenges.

Energy from the Sun

Many homes and businesses already use some passive solar energy. In other words, they maximize their use of sunlight without converting it to electricity. Modern windows, for example, let in lots of light during the day, while their insulating qualities minimize heat loss in winter and in cold regions. Some buildings also collect solar energy to help heat water or swimming pools.

In spring 2009, President Barack Obama toured a solar power site at Nellis Air Force Base in Nevada with Colonel Howard Belote (center) and Senate Majority Leader Harry Reid.

Some designers also use sunlight to improve air-conditioning efficiency, especially in humid areas. Sunlight can speed evaporation, which makes air feel less hot. Sunlight can also heat a pressurized refrigerant; the surrounding air cools when the pressure decreases.

Producing electricity from sunlight requires more complex technologies. Concentrating solar thermal technology basically collects the Sun's energy with an array of reflective materials. Lenses sometimes help concentrate the sunlight too. The area receiving the concentrated sunlight becomes extremely hot. Think about how a magnifying glass can concentrate sunlight to a point that gets hot enough to burn paper.

One type of concentrating solar thermal technology uses parabolic troughs, which are long rows of curved mirrors. A pipe running along the troughs carries hot liquid through a central area and back again. Another design uses parabolic dishes to direct the Sun's heat at a central point. Yet another type of concentrating solar thermal system aims collected sunlight from a large area to the top of a central collecting tower.

Large concentrating solar thermal systems can produce temperatures as high as 3,000 °C. Even smaller ones get hot enough to boil water. Steam from the boiling water turns turbines, which generate electricity.

Photovoltaic (PV) systems generate electricity without the intermediate step of boiling water. Sunlight strikes PV cells, which absorb some of the sunlight's energy. That energy excites electrons in the material, which causes an electric current to flow. When the sun stops striking the PV cells, the electric current stops.

In order to work, PV cells generally contain some type of semiconductor, a material that sometimes—but not always—can conduct electricity. Silicon is a familiar example, and specially prepared, high-quality crystalline silicon has traditionally been the material of choice for PV cells.

PV cells made from high-quality silicon crystals have been relatively expensive. To rein in costs, producers have tried using noncrystalline, or amorphous, silicon. So far, this material has not been as efficient at generating electricity. Thus, while each cell may be cheaper to manufacture, the overall cost per unit of electricity has not come down significantly.

Scientists and engineers are also trying PV cells made from different kinds of materials. Examples include such compounds as gallium arsenide, copper iridium diselenide, and cadmium telluride. Some researchers are also exploring whether cheap organic compounds could work well in PV cells.

Each type of PV material responds to different wavelengths of sunlight, called the material's bandwidth. Sometimes, combining two types of material with different bandwidths increases the total energy output of a PV cell. The term polycrystalline describes such cells. A higher total energy output means that polycrystalline cells can cost less per unit of electricity generated.

Thin-film deposition is another strategy for lowering the cost of PV cells. Instead of growing crystals in ingot form and then slicing them, thin-film deposition spreads electricity-generating PV material on layers of other material. Thin-film semiconductors might be less than 10 microns thick, versus 100 to 300 micrometers for PV cells made from ingot-grown crystals. Also, thin-film deposition is more suitable to automation and mass production, so each cell costs less.

A report from the Palo Alto Research Center, a subsidiary of Xerox Corporation, suggests that combining concentrating and PV systems can provide more cost savings. Basically, reflective material would concentrate sunlight onto a small area. Photovoltaic cells in those areas would then convert some of the concentrated sunlight into electricity. Layered PV cells with multiple types of semiconductor materials could convert up to 40 percent of the sunlight hitting them into electricity.

Solar energy systems do not have to be any particular size. They can be scaled up or down as circumstances require. Thus, an electric utility might run either a big or small solar energy system to help meet peak power needs. Concentrating solar thermal technology makes it easier for utilities to sell solar power. The steam-powered turbines used by those systems are similar to those used by conventional power plants.

Homes and businesses can obtain solar-generated electricity in different ways. A large business might set up an independent solar power system. Even a small home or apartment building can have rooftop solar energy equipment.

Until recently, owners of solar energy systems who were not in the business of selling electricity were the only ones who could use their systems' electricity. Solar energy equipment could reduce their bills from grid-connected electric companies, but that was about it.

Now some areas are starting to use distributed power generation. Under such arrangements, private owners of solar energy equipment can let any solar-generated electricity flow through the grid system. If the private owners wind up sending more power through the electric grid than they use, they could get a credit or other reimbursement from the utility company.

Such arrangements make solar energy systems more attractive for homes and businesses. They also help utilities meet peak power demands. Nonetheless, only limited areas offer distributed power metering. As its availability expands in the United States, people will have more incentive to add solar energy capacity to their homes and businesses.

Pros and Cons

Most environmental advocates applaud solar power. For starters, solar energy is one of the cleanest energy alternatives. As they produce electricity, solar energy facilities do not emit pollutants or greenhouse gases. (However, some energy and resources still go into manufacturing and installing the equipment.)

Solar energy is inherently renewable, since each day brings more sunlight. The flip side, of course, is that solar energy facilities stop generating energy at night. Unless scientists and engineers develop reliable ways to capture and store excess electric power on a large enough scale, most users will need some backup power for nighttime use. Advanced battery designs could potentially provide a way to store energy collected during the daylight hours.

Some solar concentrating thermal plants could also deal with the nighttime issue by using heat energy stored earlier in the day. Although the Sun will have set, the oil, molten salts, or other fluid that absorbs heat from the solar concentrators will stay hot, especially if the material is insulated well. If it were still hot enough, that heat energy might produce electricity at night.

Facilities could also switch over to natural gas for running generators at night. Burning natural gas does emit some carbon dioxide and other pollutants. However, the quantities will be lower than they would be if coal or oil powered the plant, or if a plant ran on natural gas alone.

Seasonal variations also play a role. During winter, for example, parts of Alaska and northern Europe get fewer than six hours of sunlight each day. Nevertheless, the times when solar generating facilities produce the most electricity coincide with the highest demands for electric power. During summer, for example, afternoon sunlight hours correspond roughly to times when air-conditioning needs are greatest. Even the long daylight periods in Alaska match up with increased power demands at the height of the state's tourist season. Thus, solar power's variability makes it well suited for generating electricity during times of peak demand.

Of course, the Sun does not strike the earth with the same intensity in all places. A square meter of PV cells in Phoenix, Arizona, might generate up to 7 kilowatt-hours of electricity per day. Those same PV cells would produce roughly half that much electricity in New York City. In Moscow, Russia, they would produce only 2 kilowatt-hours per day. Therefore, in areas with less intense sunlight, solar energy facilities will generally be less efficient. It will take longer for solar-generated electricity in those areas to pay back investments in equipment.

On the other hand, solar energy can provide electricity where conventional sources have not. Approximately 1.6 billion people— roughly one-fourth of the world's population—have no access to plug-in electric power. In particular, large areas of developing countries lack the infrastructure necessary to deliver electricity from central power plants. Yet even areas far from any grid can use solar technologies to meet some of their energy needs. Thus,

geography presents both benefits and disadvantages.

Area requirements for solar energy also spark debate. Solar concentrators, PV cells, and other equipment need space to collect the sun's energy. Supporters say that even a small amount of the sunlight striking our planet has the potential to generate huge amounts of electric power. As former vice president Al Gore told the Senate Foreign Relations Committee:

> [I]f we took an area of the Southwestern desert 100 miles on a side, that would be enough, in and of itself, to provide 100 percent of all the electricity needs for the United States of America in a full year.

Information from the Department of Energy supports Gore's estimate. Nonetheless, 10,000 square miles is more than the total combined land area of Rhode Island, Delaware, and Connecticut. The states of New Jersey, Vermont, Massachusetts, New Hampshire, Maryland, and Hawaii each have less than 10,000 square miles of land area too.

On the other hand, 10,000 square miles is less than 3 percent of the United States' total land area of approximately 3.5 million square miles. The country need not devote an entire 10,000 square miles to solar energy, in any case. No one type of energy is likely to supply all of the United States' electricity any time in the foreseeable future. Not even the U.S. PV industry has proposed meeting 100 percent of the country's energy needs with solar power!

Improvements in efficiency can also reduce the land area needed to generate electricity from solar energy. So far, most PV cells have converted barely one-fourth of the Sun's energy striking them into electricity. Now researchers are exploring ways to push that figure above 40 percent.

Solar panels are increasingly popular in different parts of the world.

"This technology has the potential to change the way electricity is generated throughout the world," said University of Delaware researcher Allen Barnett. In 2007 he and other researchers announced an innovative PV cell design with an energy conversion efficiency of 42.8 percent. Research projects are seeking to improve solar concentrating thermal facilities too.

Another idea for dealing with the land-area issue comes from Cool Earth Solar. This California company has suggested floating thousands of balloons with solar concentrators and PV cells inside. The company claims its concept can "reshape solar energy" by making large-scale solar energy generation practical.

Rooftop installations are a more down-to-earth example of how to deal with the area issue. Businesses and homes can install equipment on their rooftops to capture the sun. Meanwhile, people can still live and work in the buildings below. The same land area thus serves multiple purposes.

The "Bottom Line"

Sure, sunlight is free. Until recently, though, the price for solar-generated electricity has been much higher than for electricity that is generated by other means. At times, electricity from PV cells has cost more than four times that of electricity from coal-fired power plants. Compared to wind power, the price has been roughly twice as high.

The high cost of PV cells has been one reason for the high cost of solar-generated power. According to the Department of Energy, PV cell modules cost about $50 per peak watt in 1980. (A peak watt or watt peak is a measure of how much electric power a unit can produce.) By 2008 comparable costs had dropped as low as $3.

As technology advances have lowered costs for PV cells, users' bottom-line electricity prices have fallen. Advances in technology for collecting solar thermal generators will likely reduce users' prices

Solar Energy in Japan

As the twenty-first century began, Japan led the world in PV-cell production. Since then, China has built a huge PV-cell industry. Germany and Spain have also surpassed Japan in total solar energy capacity. Nevertheless, Japan continues to be a major player in the worldwide solar energy scene, and it wants to strengthen that position.

In 2008 Japan's "Action Plan for Achieving a Low-Carbon Society" announced ambitious solar energy goals:

> Japan is thus aiming to become once again the world leader in solar generation, and is promoting a huge increase in the installation of solar power generation facilities with the target of increasing the amount of installations 10-fold by 2020 and 40-fold by 2030.

> To make this increase possible, it will be necessary to bring the price down substantially through technological innovation and creation of demand. . . . With regard to price, the aim is to roughly halve the current price of a solar power generation system within three to five years.

To reach those goals, Japan's government is funding research on how to lower costs and make PV cells more efficient. The government also began offering approximately $700 in subsidies for each kilowatt of PV-generating capacity installed by homes and businesses.

Additional policy options include a feed-in tariff like the one that Germany has adopted. Such tariffs let solar energy facilities sell power back to the electricity grid for a guaranteed high price. Home and business owners thus have more incentive to add solar generating capacity.

for that electricity as well, even though that technology has its own equipment costs.

Until now, users have also had to pay almost all the costs for solar energy equipment up front. The longer users could spread out those costs over time, the lower the cost per kilowatt-hour would be. Due to perception and, in some cases, accounting considerations, most people try to spread their costs over shorter periods.

Nonetheless, solar energy prices are becoming more competitive. By 2008, the Department of Energy reported, bottom-line costs for producing PV solar energy fell to between 15 and 25 cents per kilowatt-hour. In some areas tax breaks or other government incentives have brought the figure down to 11 cents or less.

Anticipated caps on carbon emissions and other government actions will likely make coal-generated electricity less attractive in the future. Then solar energy will become more competitive in price.

Renewable Portfolio Standards and Alternative Energy Portfolio Standards should increase solar generating capacity. These are state laws or rules that require a certain amount of energy sold to come from renewable or alternative energy sources. As of 2009, all but fourteen states had adopted such standards or goals for alternative energy. The state requirements or goals give utilities an incentive to add solar energy to their portfolios—either through their own generating capacity or through distributed power options.

7 Earth, Wind, and Water

EARTH, WIND, AND WATER ARE ALL SOURCES OF
renewable energy. Geothermal power uses the heat energy from
deep within the earth to power electric turbines. Wind power uses a
variation on old-fashioned windmills. Water power takes advantage
of the force of moving water.

Each option produces little or no pollution beyond that linked
to facility construction or equipment manufacture. Yet they still
spark considerable debate.

Wind Power

People have harnessed power from the wind for more than a
thousand years. The earliest windmills had vertical sails and helped
move water or grind grain. Starting in the late thirteenth century,
European windmills began using the familiar design of sails or fan
blades rotating around a horizontal axis.

In 1888 Charles Brush of Cleveland, Ohio, coupled a windmill
with an electric generator. A few years later, in 1891, Poul la Cour
of Denmark incorporated airfoil shapes into his four-bladed windmills to boost their speed and power. Wind-powered generators
soon became very popular throughout Denmark.

By the 1920s most electricity-generating plants used fossil
fuel because it was cheap, and the plants' power output could
better meet growing demands. While some wind generators kept

operating, most could not compete with new fossil fuel plants, which were more efficient.

In 1974, soon after the Arab oil embargo, the U.S. government began its federal wind energy program. By the 1980s commercial wind farms had begun operating in California. Spread over large areas, their windmills were sometimes quite noisy.

Today's modern wind turbines are quieter, bigger, and more powerful than their 1980s counterparts. The diameter of modern wind turbines often measures more than 100 meters across. Design capabilities for wind turbines on land often range from 1.5 MW to 3.6 MW. The biggest offshore wind turbines could soon generate up to 5 MW or more.

Wind power generated about one-third of one percent of the United States' electricity in 2007. Colleges, businesses, and a growing number of residences now use wind power to replace part of their electricity needs from local utilities. Meanwhile, utilities are expanding their use of wind power for electricity production.

According to a 2008 report from the Department of Energy, wind power's share of the United States' electric energy mix could rise to 20 percent by 2030. Getting to that point will require significant expenditures. Meanwhile, critics of the technology raise several concerns.

Environmentalists want renewable energy. Yet some worry about wind power's effects on wildlife. The Center for Biological Diversity (CBD) filed a lawsuit in 2004 opposing permit renewals for the Altamont Pass Wind Resource Area (APWRA) in California's Alameda and Contra Costa counties. Since 1982, APWRA's 5,400 windmills had killed approximately 1,000 birds each year.

"Altamont Pass has become a death zone for eagles and other magnificent and imperiled birds of prey," said CBD lawyer Richard Wiebe. Jeff Miller at CBD argued that the project's location along

A model wind turbine is shown across from the Manhattan skyline at night.

a bird migration route was "the absolute worst place to put a wind farm." APWRA eventually got a permit with stricter terms, but CBD felt it did not do enough to prevent future bird deaths.

Bats have fared poorly around wind turbines, too, especially migratory species. Generally, bats use echolocation—navigation by sound—to avoid crashing into human-made structures. However, a 2008 study at the University of Calgary found that bats didn't need to crash into the turbines to be harmed by them. Air pressure changes around wind turbines can fatally harm bats' lungs. "[B]at fatalities at wind turbines far outnumber bird fatalities at most sites," noted researcher Erin Baerwald, so "wildlife fatalities at wind turbines are now a bat issue, not a bird issue."

Site permits for newer wind farm projects generally avoid migration routes. Newer wind turbines are also taller and produce more power than did earlier versions. The added height places them above some flying animals' flight paths. The extra power means that fewer turbines can generate more electricity, and so wildlife in a smaller area is at risk. Each new turbine being installed at APWRA during the coming decade will replace fifteen of the older ones.

Researchers are exploring other ways to reduce wind turbines' impact on wildlife. For example, the Bats and Wind Energy Cooperative (BWEC) began an experiment in 2008 to see whether stopping turbines during low-wind periods would reduce bat deaths. The study will also explore how temporary shutdowns might affect power generation. BWEC is an alliance among industry, government, and conservation representatives.

"I'm thrilled that this critical experiment is under way," said Merlin Tuttle of Bat Conservation International. "Our purpose is to work together on determining causes and solutions as quickly as possible."

Even under the best circumstances, wind turbines will still kill some wildlife. Nonetheless, the American Wind Energy Association [AWEA] says that it's important to keep the issue in context.

"More than a thousand times as many birds are killed flying into buildings, for example, than wind turbines," executive director Randall Swisher noted.

Meanwhile, groups such as the Sierra Club and the Audubon Society have voiced general support for wind energy. Yes, individual projects should deal appropriately with concerns about particular sites. However, the groups feel, global climate change poses even more serious risks.

"On balance, Audubon strongly supports wind power as a clean alternative energy source that reduces the threat of global warming," spokesman Mike Daulton told a congressional subcommittee in 2007. After detailing potential harm from global climate change, he added, "Our challenge is thus to help design and locate wind power projects that minimize the negative impacts on birds and wildlife."

Another problem that wind power encounters is the NIMBY syndrome. NIMBY stands for "not in my backyard." The attitude turns some people into fierce opponents of wind power when companies propose putting projects close to their homes.

Cape Wind Associates first proposed its Nantucket Sound wind power project in 2001. Its plans have called for putting 130 huge wind turbines off the shores of Cape Cod, Massachusetts. At optimum conditions, the project would produce 468 MW of electricity. Under average conditions, its expected production would be only 170 MW, yet that would still provide almost 75 percent of the average electricity demand for Cape Cod and nearby Martha's Vineyard.

Cape Wind stood to make a substantial profit. Its president, Jim Gordon, felt that the people of Massachusetts would benefit too. Cape Wind's clean, renewable energy would substantially cut down on the area's use of fossil fuels to produce electricity, while also reducing air pollution. The price consumers paid for electricity would probably drop as well.

However, some Cape Cod residents were staunchly opposed to the plan, including the late senator Edward Kennedy of Massachusetts. On clear days the wind turbines would be visible from shore, where the Kennedy family has a huge vacation compound. "The sight of them bothers me," Kennedy said in 2003. Also, he told wind-farm supporter Jim Liedell, "That's where I sail."

The senator's nephew, environmental lawyer Robert F. Kennedy Jr., also opposed the project. "As an environmentalist, I support wind power," Kennedy announced in the *New York Times.* But he felt Nantucket Sound "should be off-limits."

"This is visual pollution," objected historian David McCullough at one public meeting. Other opponents included Listerine heiress Bunny Mellon and Douglas Yearley, the former head of copper producer Phelps Dodge. Before his death in 2007, Yearley was chief executive officer for the Alliance to Protect Nantucket Sound.

The Alliance has spent millions of dollars trying to block the Cape Wind project. "Nantucket Sound: Once It's Gone, It's Gone Forever," claims one of the group's videos. The Alliance has also used legal strategies to oppose Cape Wind.

Meanwhile, other environmental groups say arguments against the wind farm are spurious. "It's really hypocritical," Barbara Hill told *The Daily Show* when asked about Senator Kennedy's stance against the project. Hill heads Clean Power Now, a nonprofit group that promotes renewable energy. As of 2007, only 14 percent of Massachusetts residents opposed the Cape Wind project.

Greenpeace USA supports the Cape Wind project too. "Now we need our leaders to do the right thing," said a 2007 Greenpeace ad, "for all the people of Massachusetts, not just for the wealthy few."

Project costs have already risen dramatically due to years of delay. Nevertheless, Cape Wind cleared an important hurdle in 2008, when the Massachusetts Department of Environmental Protection approved an application to use state waterways.

"Given that all of the applicable requirements of law have been

A group of protestors wore costumes and chanted slogans to satirize what they describe as upper-class residents of Cape Cod who are opposed to the construction of 130 windmills in Nantucket Sound.

fulfilled, we see no reason for the agency to delay issuance of the final environmental impact statement," Senate energy commission members Senators Jeff Bingaman (D-NM) and Pete Domenici (R-NM) wrote to the Department of the Interior in 2008. State and local permitting was completed, with one federal permit still needed, by late 2009."

In order for wind power to succeed long term, its price will need to be competitive with other choices, including power from fossil fuels. Prices for electricity from fossil fuels will likely increase as new regulatory programs come into effect. Nonetheless, growth in the wind energy industry will require huge investments of capital.

"Wind energy is never going to be anything but a bit player in meeting the world's energy needs," claimed the *Wall Street Journal* in a 2007 editorial. Based on construction costs for projects and prices that would be charged to consumers, the editorial's writers felt that wind power didn't make economic sense. Nor should wind power be pushed on people because it is "virtuous," they argued.

In order to meet 20 percent of the United States' energy needs, the country would need thousands more wind turbines placed over thousands of square miles. Some of those new turbines would be on land, while others would be offshore. Constructing those facilities would require major amounts of money. Even with favorable tax treatment and other incentives, expanding U.S. wind generating capacity would be expensive.

Transmitting that energy to users presents another huge challenge. As more electricity comes from wind, transmission distances will likely increase. Some prime areas for producing wind power are offshore or in remote, rural areas. Increased transmission distance means more power losses. Presently, for every 100 miles electricity must travel through transmission lines, up to 7 percent of electric power is lost. Those power losses will affect the rates consumers pay, as well as how much generating capacity the country needs.

Wind energy is also highly variable. Wind speeds change with the weather. Also, the times of peak wind energy production don't necessarily match the highest energy demands. To deal with those factors, utilities or users that rely on wind power would need some back-up electricity source. The U.S. energy distribution system would also need improvements to better handle loads and demands.

The areas where wind turbines are most effective also tend to experience severe weather, such as tornadoes or hurricanes. Such severe events can damage generating equipment. Limited availability of replacement parts can cause problems, as some colleges learned when their small wind power plants needed repair.

Despite potential problems, supporters say that wind power offers huge benefits. Creating more wind energy could improve air quality by lowering emissions of various pollutants. If wind energy made up one-fifth of the U.S. energy mix by 2030, the nation would avoid 15 billion metric tons of carbon dioxide emissions through 2050.

Remember too that wind doesn't have to be imported. Nor are

Why Denmark?
Why Not England?

By 2007 wind power was meeting 19.7 percent of Denmark's energy needs. The Danish Wind Industry Association believes that share can grow to 50 percent by 2025. The key to reaching that goal is expanding and adding power plants offshore and on land.

Danish companies have also captured a significant share of the world market for wind power equipment. The leading company, Vestas Wind Systems, had a 19.8 percent market share in 2007. By comparison, U.S.–based GE Energy had 18.6 percent, and other companies had smaller shares.

Denmark's climate and proximity to the North Sea help explain wind power's success there. Political backing and public support are just as important. To bolster that support, the Danish Wind Industry Association actively promotes the view that wind turbines are "natural elements" in the landscape. It also stresses wind energy's contributions to the country's economy.

Not all countries have been as quick to embrace wind energy. The United Kingdom (UK) also has access to the North Sea's winds, and its climate is similar to Denmark's. Yet wind power has had a slow start in the UK. Angelika Pullen, a spokeswoman for the Global Wind Energy Council, explains:

> Within Europe, the UK is a good example of a country with a huge wind resource, but which is resisting development due to lack of political will, strong lobbying from competing energy sources and strong public opinion.

Mexico, Brazil, and Chile have "great potential" too, says Pullen. "But the lack of political will and the structure of these countries' electricity markets have been slowing down development." Brazil's wind energy auction in late 2009 could signal a welcome shift for wind energy growth.

wind turbines huge targets for terrorists: an attack could interrupt service, but it wouldn't yield weapons-grade materials or cause catastrophic fires or pollution. Thus, unlike fossil fuels or nuclear power, wind energy presents few problems for national security. Supporters say this is yet another reason why the winds of change point to more wind power.

Geothermal Power: Deep-Down Energy

If your home has a furnace in the basement, pipes and ducts carry the furnace's heat to the rest of the home. Geothermal power uses a similar concept to bring heat from Earth's interior to the surface for generating power.

As depth underground increases, temperatures rise dramatically, due in part to the pressure from overlying rock. The earth's mantle, a layer from roughly 35 kilometers to 2,900 km deep, has temperatures ranging from 1,000 °C upward. The earth's core is even hotter—from 4,000 °C to more than 6,000 °C. Such intense heat comes from the radioactive decay of multiple elements, combined with residual heat from Earth's formation billions of years ago.

People can access some of the earth's deep heat in different ways. At some places that heat comes to the surface in the form of hot springs and geysers. People built the first geothermal power plant in Tuscany, Italy, in 1904. Steam from hot springs was used to power turbines that produced electricity. Geothermal power also has a long history in Iceland, where it has provided electric power for more than sixty years.

Power companies can also drill 1 to 2 miles down to access geothermal energy. A flash steam plant pumps up hot water from thousands of feet below the surface. The decrease in pressure causes the water to flash into steam, which drives the plant's electric turbines. When the steam cools, it condenses back into water. The plant then pumps it back into the deep reservoir.

A binary power plant doesn't need to pump the hot water all

the way up. Some of a deep reservoir's heat transfers to liquid run through pipes. That liquid turns to steam and powers the turbines. Either way, the geothermal energy is renewable.

Geothermal power is also reliable. The heat source is available twenty-four hours per day, without seasonal variations. Geothermal energy is shielded from most potential hazards too.

So far, most U.S. geothermal resources are in the West, where competition for water resources can become an issue. Vented gases from deep wells also cause some disputes. Hydrogen sulfide and ammonia smell bad and can cause health problems in high enough concentrations. Methane adds to greenhouse gas emissions. By comparison, though, natural gas power plants use more water and cause more gas emissions. Geothermal energy supporters say any problems are minor in comparison to the potential benefits.

According to the Energy Information Administration, the United States already leads the world in producing electricity from geothermal energy. That electricity made up barely half of one percent of all electric power produced in 2008. Also, only California, Nevada, Hawaii, and Utah had any geothermal electric plants in operation.

By 2009, though, 126 new projects were under way or in development, including facilities in nine more states. "Geothermal power projects continue to move forward, with new projects being added at an increasing rate," noted Karl Gawell, executive director of the Geothermal Energy Association. The group estimated that the new projects would supply power for more than 5 million homes. It also said the new projects would provide up to 100,000 new jobs.

So far, geothermal energy has suffered from limited investment. Many people also see it as a niche technology—suitable for certain areas but not really a widespread option. Geothermal power's small share of the energy mix has reinforced those views.

Nevertheless, a 2006 report from the Massachusetts Institute of Technology concluded that geothermal energy could produce 10 percent of the country's baseload electric needs by 2050. Nor, the report found, is the resource limited to specific geographic areas. In short, the group concluded, geothermal energy has the potential to become a "major player" in the United States. To get to that point, however, the industry will need significant expansion, plus more money for research and development.

Hydroelectric Power

Waterwheel technology dates back to ancient times, so it's no surprise that the United States has used hydroelectric power since the 1880s. More than 70 percent of the country's renewable energy came from hydroelectric plants in 2007. Overall, hydropower accounts for 6 percent of all electricity generated in the United States. The proportion of hydropower varies from state to state, however. In Idaho, for example, hydroelectric plants provide about four-fifths of all electricity.

Most hydropower plants use water flowing from one elevation to another. Flowing water turns metal blades and powers an electric generator. Waterfalls make great locations, as the Niagara Falls generating plants show.

Dams across rivers are also good places for hydroelectric generators. Good examples include the Hoover Dam across the Colorado River and the Grand Coulee Dam across the Columbia River. Water enters sluice gates, channels with valves to regulate flow, on the reservoir side of a dam. The water flows down through another channel to the metal blades. The spinning motion works an electric generator that sits above the blades. Electricity flows out from a powerhouse on top of the dam. Flowing water exits the dam at a level lower than it entered and keeps flowing downstream.

While power demands vary throughout the day and night, water flows through a hydroelectric plant at a fairly constant rate. To cope with peaks in demand, some hydroelectric plants have

A hydroelectric power plant in Niagara Falls, Ontario, Canada.

pumped storage as part of their design. At times when electricity demand is lower than supply, the plant pumps some water up to a separate storage tank at a higher elevation. When demand is high, the plant lets water flow down from the pumped storage reservoir to turn a turbine.

Overall, hydroelectric power is reliable. The price to end users is also relatively low, once construction costs for the power plant and any dams are paid. Because the flowing water is free, the marginal cost for hydroelectric power can also be cheaper than that from fossil fuel plants. (In economics, marginal cost is the added expense for producing one additional unit of something.)

Of course, hydropower requires a source of water that can flow from one level to another. Thus, it has some geographic limitations. Water flow also tends to vary on a seasonal basis. Most plants deal with this by adjusting the sluice gates to let more or less water through.

103

Generating hydroelectric power does not give off air pollution, so it does not present a breathing hazard or add to global climate change once a plant is in operation. Hydroelectric power does not contaminate water, either. Moreover, the dams that work with hydroelectric plants often have other purposes, such as aiding in the irrigation of farmland. In some cases dams built to generate hydroelectric power have even created recreational areas, such as Lake Mead, a human-made lake in Arizona and Nevada.

Hydroelectric plants are not ideal. The dams that create reservoirs change landscapes and wildlife habitats. However, design modifications can reduce the harm they do. For example, some hydroelectric plants have so-called fish ladders. They create a path for migrating fish, such as salmon, to swim upstream to their spawning grounds.

Hydroelectric power also requires significant space for dams and reservoirs, which may compete with existing or potential land uses. China's Three Gorges Dam started generating electricity in 2003 and is now the world's largest hydroelectric power project. Building the project displaced more than 1.2 million people.

Hydroelectric power will probably continue to expand in China, Brazil, and various developing countries. Due to space limitations, power companies probably won't construct huge hydroelectric plants at new locations in the United States. However, only a fraction of the country's existing dams have hydropower generators. Most have functions, such as for irrigation, or as reservoirs. Adding hydroelectric generators to some of those existing dams could add renewable energy capacity, especially in smaller communities.

Current from Currents

Twice daily, billions of gallons of water flow into and out from the country's ocean coastlines. Tidal power uses the force of that water to produce electricity. Electricity production has twice-daily peaks and lows, depending on local conditions.

Early tidal plant designs used barrages. Barrages resemble hydroelectric plant dams, except they're built on part of a tidal bay or estuary. The La Rance project, near Normandy, France, generates up to 240 MW. The Annapolis Tidal Generating Station in Nova Scotia's Bay of Fundy is another huge project. "This plant produces on average 30 gigawatt-hours of renewable green energy per year," says Robert Duran, the superintendent for Fundy Tidal. (One gigawatt equals 1,000 MW.) The Annapolis plant's output "would supply 5,000 homes with electrical energy for a year using 6,000 kilowatts as a yearly average household consumption."

Tidal basins and estuaries provide homes for many species. Damming up parts of the area can adversely affect water flow and

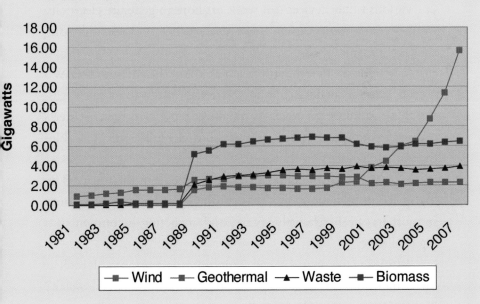

Installed Renewable Generation Capacity— Selected Sources

Source: Energy Information Administration, "Installed Renewable Generation Capacity, 1981-2007," data released 2009, http://www.eia.doe.gov/oiaf/aeo/otheranalysis/aeo_2009analysispapers/excel/figure21_data.xls

other habitat features. Navigation safety is also a concern. Coastal areas' changing features present problems too. Wave action washes sand and other debris away from parts of the coast and deposits them elsewhere. Barrages can interfere with that process.

Tidal turbines provide a less intrusive option than barrages. They look like short windmills or giant propellers that work underwater. Because water flows through and around them, tidal turbines have less impact on coastal areas than barrages do. Careful design and positioning should ensure the turbines do not interfere with navigation and minimize contact with marine life.

The world's first grid-connected set of tidal turbines is already at work in New York Harbor. In 2008 Verdant Power completed its six-turbine, 80-MW Roosevelt Island Tidal Energy (RITE) demonstration project. Work is now underway to expand the RITE project. Other tidal turbine projects are under way in North America and elsewhere.

Various other devices can work offshore to generate electricity from ocean currents. Some wave-power generators resemble long snakes. Examples include the Pelamis by Pelamis Wave Power and the Anaconda by Checkmate Seaenergy. Another design, by AWS Ocean Energy, anchors buoys underwater with pressurized gas. For these and other generators, the motion of passing waves exerts pressure, which the devices convert into electrical energy. Cables carry that electricity to shore.

Marine energy will almost certainly expand in the future. The big question is how quickly that can happen. So far, government support has been relatively sparse, and attracting investment is a big challenge.

Permitting requirements can complicate matters more. "It took us more than four years to get approval to put six turbines in the water," Verdant Power's Trey Taylor told *Environmental Health Perspectives* magazine. Inevitably, such delays drive up expenses. Meanwhile, customers wait longer to use new sources of alternative energy.

$\boxed{8}$ Moving Forward

ONE WAY OR ANOTHER, MORE OF THE UNITED
States' electricity and transportation power will come from alternative energy sources in the coming decades. Yet solving the country's energy problems will take more than mixing a medley of technologies.

Good to Go?

Consumers will embrace alternative energy options for transportation only if they have practical and affordable choices for getting around. Such choices would include innovative automobiles that can use different energy technologies, plus convenient ways to refuel them.

Hybrid cars are already doing well in the market. Basically, they add an electric generator to a gasoline-powered engine. While the car runs on gasoline or diesel fuel, it also generates and stores electricity during part of the drive. The rest of the time, the car can draw on that electrical energy for power.

Some hybrids already average more than 40 miles per gallon of gasoline. Federal fuel-efficiency standards adopted in 2009 require cars and light trucks to average at least 35.5 miles per gallon by 2016. That requirement and other rules should inspire automakers to market more fuel-efficient hybrids.

Driving a practical car that uses little or no fossil fuels at all is more difficult. More than 4 million flex-fuel vehicles were on U.S.

A Tesla Roadster is electrically charged at Tesla Motors in San Carlos, California.

roads in 2007. However, more than 99 percent still used regular gasoline, because E85 fuel and service stations were so scarce. Moreover, when the federal government added more than 100,000 flex-fuel vehicles to agency fleets, some of those vehicles wound up using more gasoline than the vans or trucks they had replaced. If policy makers want biofuels to function as practical alternative fuels instead of just additives, American drivers need both the vehicles and convenient ways to fuel them.

Hydrogen fuel cell cars are not available for purchase in the U.S. mass market; nor is it clear if or when they ever will be. Electric cars date back to the 1890s, although gasoline-powered vehicles became cheaper and more practical to run. Concerns about fuel economy and environmental issues renewed interest in electric cars during the 1990s.

For example, Ford introduced its TH!NK electric car model, and General Motors came out with its EV1. Within just a few years, though, the automakers stopped making both cars. "The electric-vehicle market failed to materialize, not for lack of effort but for lack of customers willing to sacrifice the utility of today's gasoline-powered vehicles," GM representative Sam Leonard said in 2000. The company argued that customers viewed gasoline-powered vehicles as more useful and practical.

"They're the cleanest cars ever made, and they want to take them off the road," motorist Greg Hanssen told *Salon*. "It just baffles." Of course, the type of energy that charges an electric vehicle battery determines how clean it really is. If that energy comes from alternative fuel sources, though, many environmentalists agree that an electric vehicle would be cleaner than a gasoline-powered one.

Furor over fuel prices and improvements in vehicle batteries have spurred new interest in electric vehicles. Despite improved performance, it is unclear how soon price and other factors will make electric vehicles practical for many buyers. In 2009, for example, the high-performance Tesla Roadster had a price tag of more than $100,000. The expected price tag for General Motors' 2010 Volt was about $40,000, but the Volt drew criticism even before GM filed for bankruptcy in 2009. Even with possible tax credits, its design and price compared poorly to hybrids already on the road.

Think Global, a Norwegian firm, started selling the TH!NK City electric car in the United States in 2009 with a more modest price of less than $25,000. Ford, Chrysler, Toyota, Nissan, and BMW have been developing electric cars, too, and could soon introduce their models. If sticker tags run higher than conventional cars, though, that might still deter many buyers. "Gas prices would have to go to $8 a gallon before the average buyer sees an electric vehicle as a sensible option," Michael Omotoso of J. D. Power and Associates told *Fortune* magazine.

Public transportation systems have been somewhat further ahead in experimenting with alternative fuels. Many buses now run on liquefied natural gas, for example. While it's still a fossil fuel, it burns cleaner and produces less greenhouse gas than conventional diesel fuel.

Of course, if more people rode public transit, overall dependence on fossil fuels would go down. Getting more people to use public transit presents a "chicken and egg" problem. Public transit is not a practical option in areas that have inadequate networks or that have not kept up with changing patterns of where people live and work. Unless transit authorities are sure they will have sufficient riders and revenues, however, most hesitate to expand or upgrade their systems.

Improving public transit would help address the country's energy concerns in the area of transportation. Even with income from fares, however, public transit programs must compete for limited tax dollars. Getting that money is an even bigger challenge in tough economic times.

Gearing Up for the Smart Grid

"On any given day, 500,000 people are temporarily without electricity," reported Clark Gellings of the Electric Power Research Institute. When it comes to electricity, the country needs a massive overhaul for its grid—the system for getting electrical power from points of generation to users across the country. Unless the country makes changes soon, the grid's problems will worsen as alternative energy use grows.

With today's grid, seemingly minor incidents can trigger major problems. On August 14, 2003, for example, overgrown trees came into contact with electrical wires in northeastern Ohio. The local power company did not respond appropriately, which caused short circuits. The short circuits triggered a cascading blackout. Like falling dominoes, two hundred sixty-five power plants shut down. Fifty million people in the United States and Canada lost electric power.

As the 2003 blackout showed, millions of people's everyday activities can come to a halt when the electricity delivery system fails. Think of the United States' electric grid as one of the world's largest interconnected machines. "It's technologically complex," says Mark Bello, a spokesman for the National Institute of Standards and Technology. "It's also complex from a regulatory standpoint."

For starters, the grid includes 5.4 million miles of distribution and transmission cables. "So you could circle the Earth at the equator more than 200 times with that length of cable," says Bello. Add in 22,000 substations and 130 million watt-power meters spread out through fifty states and the District of Columbia, and you have a massive system.

Despite its complexity, the U.S. power grid is basically one hundred years old. Moreover, even a small percentage of outages is no longer acceptable. A study by the Lawrence Berkeley National Laboratory in California estimated that power interruptions cost the country approximately $80 billion each year.

The grid works best when all connected generators and transmission systems work in synchrony. However, variability is inherent in how people get and use electricity. "Basically, the amount of power being consumed by customers in any given area has to be exactly synchronous, or the same, as the amount being generated," Jim Owen at the Edison Electric Institute explained. Otherwise, lines can overheat, or fires or other problems can occur. "There has to be a perfect balance, because you can't store electricity."

Sudden jumps in demand can cause instability. Similarly, sudden decreases in the ability to meet demand produce instability. If the system can't compensate, shutoffs occur, and areas lose power. In many cases power companies don't know that failures have happened until a customer calls to say the lights are out.

Growing reliance on alternative energy can aggravate the issue. After all, wind power generation changes with the weather. Solar energy varies with the time of day, weather, and season. "As more and more of your electric power usage comes from those kinds of variable sources," says Bello, "the more vulnerable the grid becomes to becoming unstable."

The solution is a modernized electricity network known as the smart grid. One aim of the smart grid movement is to give power companies real-time feedback on systems operations. Beyond that, digital controls and other switching equipment will balance loads and improve efficiency.

The smart grid movement will also make electric power more portable. Currently, says Bello, "The distribution of renewable sources, wind and solar in particular, is pretty much limited to the area where it's produced." Besides improving stability and efficiency, a smart grid will let all parts of the electric grid communicate with each other.

For example, electricity produced at a wind farm in North Dakota might go to more heavily populated areas. Transmission distance would still cause some significant losses. However, the smart grid's improvements in stability and efficiency would cut those losses by 30 percent. This could significantly improve the costs and feasibility of transmitting power over longer distances.

Smart grid plans also call for more sophisticated metering. That step would make distributed generation more practical, so small wind farms and rooftop solar panels could feed into the national grid. The overall energy supply would increase, and equipment owners would get paid for any power they supply.

During the August 14, 2003, blackout in New York City, the sidewalks of Manhattan came alive. Some people slept, some talked, and some even danced the dark night away.

Sophisticated metering would also give customers more incentive to conserve energy. The first step would be to charge for actual usage, based on demand and cost at that time of day. Customers might opt to let certain appliances run automatically only at the lowest-cost times.

Making smart grid improvements won't be cheap. It cost about $100 million for a pilot program in Boulder, Colorado, to install approximately 25,000 smart meters. Besides meters, utilities will need to spend significant amounts for state-of-the-art equipment for their plants, substations, and other parts of the system. Additionally, the electric industry needs to develop and implement national standards, so the system can work as a national grid, versus the regional systems that exist today.

According to the Electric Power Research Institute, paying for the smart grid could cost $13 billion a year for twenty years. That's two-thirds more than the industry currently invests annually. The economic stimulus package that Congress passed in 2009 included $4.5 billion to jump-start the smart grid. Much remains to be done, yet Department of Energy Secretary Chu is convinced the effort is worthwhile:

> The Smart Grid is an urgent national priority that requires all levels of government as well as industry to cooperate. . . . We still have much to do, but the ultimate result will be a much more efficient, flexible power grid and the opportunity to dramatically increase our use of renewable energy.

Saving Energy

Energy conservation will not eliminate the need for alternative energy sources. However, it can help limit growing demand. Conservation can save money and other limited resources. Conservation and better efficiency can also help mitigate, or lessen, any effects from global climate change.

Public and private initiatives promote conservation in numerous ways. For example, the federal government's Energy Star program encourages the sale of energy-efficient appliances, home improvements, electronic devices, and new homes. The voluntary program by the Environmental Protection Agency and Department of Energy lets manufacturers display the Energy Star label if they meet specific standards. Consumers see the label as a sign that they can save on energy costs. For certain categories, such as water heaters, purchases may also qualify for tax credits.

The Clean Cities program aims to reduce petroleum fuel use by motor vehicles. The Department of Energy's Clean Cities program promotes alternative energy among thousands of entities, including state and local agencies, commercial truck and bus fleets, public transit authorities, and private groups. Among other things, Clean Cities promotes alternative fuel vehicles, such as buses that run on liquefied natural gas. The program also discourages vehicle idling, which uses fuel and adds to air pollution.

Other programs encourage energy-saving and environmentally friendly buildings. For example, the Lawrence Berkeley National Laboratory has a building technologies program that conducts research and shares results with the public. Private groups, such as the nonprofit U.S. Green Building Council, also share information and encourage certification of buildings that meet its engineering and architecture standards.

Individuals can also take steps to save energy in their daily activities. Conservation on a personal level often has added benefits too. Walking instead of driving can provide the benefits of physical exercise. A compact fluorescent light bulb can save approximately $30 in energy over the course of its lifetime, according to the Energy Star program.

Issues dealing with alternative energy will remain open for debate for years to come. The more energy we can save through conservation, the less there will be to argue about.

Commuters hold on to a pole in a crowded subway car.

Tips to Save Energy

Almost everyone can do something to save energy. Here are some ways to make a difference in your personal life:

- Walk or ride your bike. Your family will save money on fuel costs, and you'll reap the benefits of extra aerobic exercise.
- Use mass transit more often. The bus or train is probably already going your way.
- Carpool when possible.
- When your family uses the car, combine trips whenever possible and avoid prolonged periods of idling.
- Turn things off! Turn off lights, computers, and other items when no one is using them. Unplug cell phone and battery chargers as soon as they've finished their jobs.
- Be smart about appliance use. Run the dishwasher when it has a full load, and let dishes air dry instead of using the heat cycle. Decide what you want to eat before opening the refrigerator, instead of letting the cool air escape while you make up your mind. Avoid heating up the kitchen by using the microwave instead of the oven to reheat food. Use a lid when boiling water; it saves energy, and the water heats faster.

- Shop smart. Try compact fluorescent bulbs instead of standard bulbs. Consider energy savings when it's time to buy a car, home appliance, or improvement for your home.
- Let the light shine in—or not! When it's cold out, open the curtains so the Sun's heat can help warm your home. Closing the curtains in hot weather can help your room stay cooler.
- Keep your cool. Set the thermostat a few degrees higher than usual in summer to save on air-conditioning costs, and turn off the air conditioner when no one is home. Set the thermostat a bit lower than usual in the winter, and wear a sweater to chase away chills.
- Don't waste water! You'll help your town or city save energy on pumping water. Besides, water is a precious resource in its own right. Turn off water while brushing your teeth.
- Know when to go low-tech. If you're able-bodied, for example, rake leaves instead of using a leaf blower.

Notes

Chapter 1

p. 5, "In a 2009 survey by the . . .": Pew Research Center for the People & the Press, "Economy, Jobs Trump All Other Policy Priorities in 2009," January 22, 2009, http://people-press.org/report/485/economy-top-policy-priority (accessed January 29, 2009).

p. 5, "In another survey by the Chicago . . .": Chicago Council on Global Affairs, "Anxiety Over Energy, Jobs, and Wealth Shakes America's Global Economic Confidence," October 14, 2008, 3, www.thechicagocouncil.org/UserFiles/File/POS_Topline%20 Reports/POS%202008/2008%20Public%20Opinion_Economic. pdf (accessed January 29, 2009).

p. 5, "The Energy Information Administration predicts . . .": Energy Information Administration, "World Energy Demand and Economic Outlook," May 27, 2009, www.eia.doe.gov/oiaf/ieo/ world.html (accessed October 28, 2009).

p. 6, "In July of 2008 the nationwide average . . .": Paul Davidson, "Officials Probe Charges of Gas-Price Gouging," *USA Today*, September 17, 2008, 4B.

p. 6, "An oil crisis is coming . . .": Roger Lowenstein, "What Price Oil?" *New York Times Magazine*, October 19, 2008, 46, 48.

p. 6, "Gas prices are killing folks . . .": Aswini Anburajan, "Obama Talks Gas Prices," April 1, 2008, http://firstread.msnbc.msn.com/ archive/2008/04/01/848005.aspx (accessed September 1, 2009).

p. 6, "Long-term," McCain added, "we've got to become . . .": Associated Press, "Obama Slams McCain, Bush on Economy," June 9, 2008, www.usatoday.com/news/politics/election2008/2008-06-09-campaign-monday_N.htm (accessed September 1, 2009).

p. 7, "It may be a little harder politically . . .": Asjylyn Loder, "Is Obama's Energy Policy a Cure for Oil Addiction?" November 23, 2008, www.tampabay.com/news/business/energy/article912737.ece (accessed January 8, 2009); Josh Dorner, "Obama Hits Green Homerun with Remarks to Govs on Energy, Climate," November 18,2008,www.huffingtonpost.com/josh-dorner/obama-hits-green-homerun_b_144691.html (accessed January 8, 2009); Business Council on Sustainable Energy, "President-elect Obama on US Energy Policy: It's More Important Now," November 17, 2008, www.bcse.org/images/pdf/bcse%20press%20release%20 11_17_08.pdf (accessed January 8, 2009).

p. 7, "Now we have a choice . . .": Jimmy Carter, "Address to the Nation on Energy," April 18, 1977, http://millercenter.org/scripps/archive/speeches/detail/3398 (accessed January 8, 2009); Jimmy Carter, "The President's Proposed Energy Policy," April 18, 1977, www.pbs.org/wgbh/amex/carter/filmmore/ps_energy.html (accessed June 5, 2009).

p. 7–8, "Now the United States has grown . . .": Energy Information Administration, "How Dependent Are We on Foreign Oil?" April 23, 2009, http://tonto.eia.doe.gov/energy_in_brief/foreign_oil_depen dence.cfm (accessed August 4, 2009); Energy Information Admin- istration, "Crude Oil FAQs," 2007–2009, http://tonto.eia.doe.gov/ ask/crudeoil_faqs.asp (accessed August 4, 2009).

p. 8, "Canada and Mexico have consistently . . .": Energy Information Association, "Crude Oil and Total Petroleum Imports, Top 15 Countries," December 29, 2008, www.eia.doe.gov/pub/oil_gas/petroleum/data_publications/company_level_imports/current/import.html (accessed January 8, 2009).

p. 8, "America is addicted to oil . . .": George W. Bush, "State of the Union Address by the President," January 31, 2006, www.whitehouse.gov/stateoftheunion/2006/ (accessed January 8, 2009).

pp. 8–9, "We've got to stop sending $700 billion . . .": Commission on Presidential Debates, Debate Transcript, October 15, 2008, www.debates.org/pages/trans2008d.html (accessed January 9, 2008).

p. 9, "Warming of the climate system is . . .": Intergovernmental Panel on Climate Change (IPCC), "Climate Change 2007—Synthesis Report: Summary for Policymakers," November 2007, 2, 5, 10, www.ipcc.ch/pdf/assessment-report/ar4/syr/ar4_syr_spm.pdf (accessed January 12, 2009).

p. 9, "average global temperatures will . . .": IPCC Working Group I, "Climate Change 2007—The Physical Science Basis: Summary for Policymakers," 13, www.ipcc.ch/pdf/assessment-report/ar4/wg1/ar4-wg1-spm.pdf (accessed January 12, 2009).

p. 11, "We don't know exactly how serious . . .'" Mark Levine, interview by Kathiann M. Kowalski, August 23, 2007.

p. 13, "We, the human species, are confronting . . .": Al Gore, "Nobel Lecture," December 10, 2007, http://nobelprize.org/nobel_prizes/peace/laureates/2007/gore-lecture_en.html (accessed January 12, 2009).

p. 14, "President Bush announced in 2001 . . .": Public Broadcasting Service, "Online NewsHour: Bush and the Environment," March 29, 2001, www.pbs.org/newshour/bb/environment/jan-june01/bushenv_3-29.html (accessed May 26, 2009).

p. 16, "In December 2009, the world's. . .": Jeffrey Ball, "Summit Leaves Key Questions Unresolved," *Wall Street Journal,* December 21, 2009, p. A17.

p. 16, "Shortly before the Copenhagen . .": White House, "President To Attend Copenhagen Climate Talks," November 25, 2009, www.whitehouse.gov/the-press-office/president-attend-copenhagen-climate-talks (accessed December 29, 2009).

p. 16, "Even if Congress did not pass any. . .": Environmental Protection Agency, "Endangerment and Cause or Contribute Findings for Greenhouse Gases under the Clean Air Act," December 7, 2009, www.epa.gov/climatechange/endangerment. html (accessed December 29, 2009), citing *Massachusetts* v. *EPA*, 549 U.S. 497 (2007).

p. 17, "By August 2009, 14.9 million people . . .": U.S. Bureau of Labor Statistics, "The Employment Situation—August 2009," September 4, 2009, www.bls.gov/news.release/pdf/empsit.pdf (accessed September 4, 2009).

p. 17, "Obama himself announced a goal . . .": Obama for America, "Barack Obama's Plan to Create 5 Million New Green Jobs," 2008, http://obama.3cdn.net/eff0ff1daa8bafe984_4yjqmv8j3.pdf (accessed September 1, 2009); Marla Dickerson, "Why Obama's Green Jobs Plan Might Work," January 4, 2009, http://articles.la times.com/2009/jan/04/business/fi-greenjobs4 (accessed September 1, 2009).

p. 18, "The International Energy Agency (IEA) . . .": International Energy Agency/Organisation for Economic Co-operation and Development, *World Energy Outlook 2008*, Paris: International Energy Agency, 2008, 3, 28–32.

p. 18, "We must usher in a global energy . . .": International Energy Agency, "New Energy Realities—WEO Calls for Global Energy Revolution Despite Economic Crisis," November 12, 2008, www. iea.org/Textbase/press/pressdetail.asp?PRESS_REL_ID=275 (accessed May 27, 2009).

p. 19, "CRA International, a consulting firm . . .": Jeffrey Ball, "Does Green Energy Add 5 Million Jobs?" *Wall Street Journal*, November 7, 2008, A13, http://online.wsj.com/article/ SB122601449992806743.html (accessed September 1, 2009).

p. 19, "Reports from the Natural Resources . . .": Natural Resources Defense Council, "Clean-Energy Investment Provides Economic Boost, More Jobs, and Expanded Opportunities," June 18, 2009, www.

nrdc.org/media/2009/090618.asp (accessed September 1, 2009).

p. 19, "It's never been clearer . . .": Natural Resources Defense Council, "Clean-Energy Investment Provides Economic Boost, More Jobs, and Expanded Opportunities," June 18, 2009.

p. 21, "By August . . .": U.S. Bureau of Labor Statistics, "The Employment Situation—August 2009," September 4, 2009, www.bls.gov/news.release/pdf/empsit.pdf (accessed September 4, 2009).

Chapter 2

p. 26, "'Drill, baby, drill!' The chant echoed . . .": "The Truth about Drilling," *USA Today*, September 9, 2008.

p. 26, "the Union of Concerned Scientists reports . . .": Union of Concerned Scientists, "How Natural Gas Works," 2009, www.ucsusa.org/clean_energy/technology_and_impacts/energy_technologies/how-natural-gas-works.html (accessed February 4, 2010).

p. 27, "As of 2007 natural gas . . .": Energy Information Administration, "Natural Gas—A Fossil Fuel," 2008, www.eia.doe.gov/kids/energyfacts/sources/non-renewable/naturalgas.html#WHAT%20IT%20IS%20USED%20FOR (accessed March 2, 2009).

p. 27, "One study from Sweden's Uppsala University . . .": Graham Jones, "World Oil and Gas 'Running Out,'" *CNN.com*, October 2, 2003, www.cnn.com/2003/WORLD/europe/10/02/global.warming/ (accessed March 2, 2009).

p. 27, "After any peak, the British Broadcasting Corporation (BBC) . . .": Will Smale, "The World's Overflowing Oil Reserves?" British Broadcasting Corporation News, April 20, 2004, http://news.bbc.co.uk/2/hi/business/3590137.stm (accessed March 2, 2009).

p. 27, "more optimistic view came from . . .": Carl Mortished, "World Not Running Out of Oil, Say Experts," *Times* Online, January 18, 2008, http://business.timesonline.co.uk/tol/business/industry_sectors/natural_resources/article3207311.ece (accessed March 2, 2009).

pp. 27–28, "Polls in 2008 showed roughly 70 percent . . .": American Petroleum Institute, "Poll: Voters Support Offshore Development," February 23, 2009, www.api.org/Newsroom/voters_support.cfm (accessed September 1, 2009).

p. 28, "Republican Newt Gingrich, a former . . .": Newt Gingrich with Vince Haley, *Drill Here, Drill Now, Pay Less: A Handbook for Slashing Gas Prices and Solving Our Energy Crisis*, Washington, DC: Regnery Publishing, 2008, 13–21.

p. 28, "Critics contend that increased drilling . . .": Bryan Walsh, "Will More Drilling Mean Cheaper Gas?" *Time* Online, June 18, 2008, www.time.com/time/business/article/0,8599,1815884,00. html (accessed March 2, 2009).

p. 28, "What the nation needs is a policy . . .": American Petroleum Institute, "Oral Statement of API Chairman Larry Nichols on Behalf of the American Petroleum Institute before the House Natural Resources Committee," February 25, 2009, www.api.org/ Newsroom/upload/API_Chairman_Larry_Nichols_Statement.pdf (accessed October 22, 2009).

pp. 28–29, "The API argues that the environmental . . .": American Petroleum Institute, "Second to None: The U.S. Offshore Industry's Safety and Environmental Records," July 15, 2008, www.api.org/ aboutoilgas/sectors/explore/secondtonone.cfm (accessed March 2, 2009).

p. 29, "In 1989 the *Exxon Valdez* . . .": National Oceanic and Atmospheric Administration, "Office of Exxon Valdez Oil Spill (EVOS) Damage Assessment and Restoration," www.fakr.noaa.gov/ oil/default.htm (accessed March 2, 2009); Wesley Loy, "Guarding against Another Valdez," *Anchorage Daily News*, March 24, 2009, http://spillcontainment.wordpress.com/2009/03/24/guarding-against-another-exxon-valdez/ (accessed August 6, 2009).

p. 29, "still opposed drilling in the Arctic National . . .": National Resources Defense Council, "Arctic National Wildlife Refuge: Why Trash an American Treasure for a Tiny Percentage of Our

Oil Needs?" www.nrdc.org/land/wilderness/arctic.asp#col-main (accessed March 2, 2009).

p. 29, "Oil and natural gas are the indispensable . . .": American Petroleum Institute, "Letter of Red Cavaney to Members of Congress," June 29, 2007, www.api.org/Newsroom/upload/rc_moc_6_29_07.pdf (accessed March 2, 2009).

p. 29, "As of 2009 coal produced approximately half . . .": Energy Information Administration, "Electric Power Monthly—Executive Summary," February 2009, www.eia.doe.gov/cneaf/electricity/epm/epm_sum.html (accessed March 2, 2009).

p. 29, "Coal is a black, solid material that contains . . .": Department of Energy, "Coal—A Fossil Fuel," 2008, www.eia.doe.gov/kids/energyfacts/sources/non-renewable/coal.html (accessed June 5, 2009).

p. 30, "older coal plants remain a concern for . . .": Sierra Club, "Dirty Coal Power," 2008, www.sierraclub.org/cleanair/factsheets/power.asp (accessed February 24, 2009).

p. 32, "The average efficiency of coal-fired power . . .": Keith Bradsher, "China Outpaces U.S. in Cleaner Coal-fired Plants," May 10, 2009, www.nytimes.com/2009/05/11/world/asia/11coal.html (accessed August 7, 2009); Siemens AG, "Coal-fired Power Plant with 50% Efficiency Rating," 2008, http://w1.siemens.com/innovation/en/news_events/ct_pressemitteilungen/index/e_research_news/2008/index/e_22_resnews_0814_2.htm (accessed August 7, 2009); EurActiv.com, "Analysis: Efficiency of Coal-fired Power Stations—Evolution and Prospects," April 25, 2006, www.euractiv.com/en/energy/analysis-efficiency-coal-fired-power-stations-evolution-prospects/article-154672 (accessed August 7, 2009).

p. 32, "enough coal to last at least two .": Cathy Booth Thomas, "Is Coal Golden?" *Time*, October 2, 2006, www.time.com/time/magazine/article/0,9171,1541270-1,00.html (accessed February 24, 2009).

p. 32, "It is imperative that we figure out a . . .": Department of Energy, "Clean Coal Technology & the Clean Coal Power Initiative," 2009, http://fossil.energy.gov/programs/powersystems/cleancoal/ (accessed February 25, 2009).

p. 33, "More than 70 percent of our power . . .": Ma Amin, interview by Kathiann M. Kowalski, August 24, 2007.

p. 34, "If we've got the oil and gas in these . . .": Jeannette J. Lee, "Big Oil Likes Clean Coal," *National Journal*, October 24, 2008, 6.

p. 35, "Within the United States coal-burning . . .": H. Joseph Herbert, "Power Plant CO_2 Increases by 3 Percent," *USA Today*, March 8, 2008, www.usatoday.com/news/nation/2008-03-18-357 8922314_x.htm (accessed February 25, 2009).

p. 35, "William Sweet has suggested that similar . . .": William Sweet, *Kicking the Carbon Habit: Global Warming and the Case for Renewable and Nuclear Energy*, New York: Columbia University Press, 2006, 143.

p. 36, "Other critics of sequestration, such as the . . .": Barbara Freese, Steve Clemmer, and Alan Nogee, "Coal Power in a Warming World: A Sensible Transition to Cleaner Energy Options," Union of Concerned Scientists, October 2008, 15–16, www.ucsusa.org/assets/documents/clean_energy/Coal-power-in-a-warming-world.pdf (accessed March 4, 2009).

p. 36, "deep groundwater supplies below . . .": Werner Aeschbach-Hertig, "Clean Coal and Sparkling Water," *Nature*, April 2, 2009, 583–584.

p. 36, "Yet another strategy for making. . .": "Greenhouse Gas Villain Rehabbed," *USA Today*, February 25, 2009, 3B.

p. 36, "In one 2008 report the consulting firm . . .": McKinsey & Company, "Carbon Capture & Storage: Assessing the Economics," 2008, www.mckinsey.com/clientservice/ccsi/pdf/CCS_Assessing_the_Economics.pdf (accessed February 25, 2009); Eoin O'Carroll, "What Is Clean Coal Anyway?" *Christian Science Monitor*, October

17, 2008, http://features.csmonitor.com/environment/2008/10/17/ what-is-clean-coal-anyway/ (accessed February 25, 2009).

p. 37, "There is no such thing as clean coal . . .'": James Hansen, Energy Action Coalition teleconference, September 11, 2008; SustainableBusiness.com, "No Clean Coal Campaign Insists on the Truth," December 11, 2008, www.sustainablebusiness.com/index. cfm/go/news.display/id/17299 (accessed February 25, 2009).

p. 37, "The Reality Coalition, an alliance . . .": Reality Coalition, "This Is Reality," 2008, www.thisisreality.org/#/?p=facility (accessed February 25, 2009).

p. 37, "In 2003 the Department of Energy announced . . .": Wyatt Andrews, "Clean Coal—Pipe Dream or Next Big Thing?" CBS News, June 20, 2008, www.cbsnews.com/stories/2008/06/20/ eveningnews/main4199506.shtml (accessed February 25, 2009).

p. 37, "Just five years later the government . . .": Thomas F. Armistead, "DOE Drops Clean-Coal Plant to Focus on Carbon Capture," *ENR: Engineering News-Record*, February 11, 2008, 12.

p. 37, "FutureGen should have been called . . .": James Hansen, Energy Action Coalition teleconference, September 10, 2008.

pp. 37–39, "Even if coal capture and storage works . . .": Union of Concerned Scientists, "So-Called 'Clean Coal' Technology Offers Promise Along with Considerable Risks, New Report Finds," October 15, 2008, www.ucsusa.org/news/press_release/coal-power-warming-world-0151.html (accessed March 4, 2009).

Chapter 3

p. 41, "Up to 15 billion gallons per year . . .": Rebecca Coons, "Study Finds Refineries Can Meet Biofuel Mandate Using Cellulosic Feedstock," *Chemical Week*, February 16/23, 2009, 9; Biotechnology Industry Organization, "New Study Shows Large Volumes of Cellulosic Biofuels Can Be Sustainably Produced by 2030," February 10, 2009, www.bio.org/news/pressreleases/newsitem. asp?id=2009_0210_01 (accessed April 17, 2009).

p. 43, "more than 11 billion gallons. . .": Angela Neville, "Texas Loses 'Food v. Fuel' Biofuel Feud," *Power*, October 2008, 32.

p. 43, "ethanol tax incentives caused the . . .": Congressional Budget Office, "The Impact of Ethanol Use on Food Prices and Greenhouse Gas Emissions," April 2009, 2, www.cbo.gov/ ftpdocs/100xx/doc10057/04-08-Ethanol.pdf (accessed April 14, 2009); Jeff Siegel with Chris Nelder and Nick Hodge, *Investing in Renewable Energy: Making Money on Green Chip Stocks*, Hoboken, NJ: John Wiley & Sons, 2008, 156–159; Marianne Lavelle and Bret Schulte, "Is Ethanol the Answer?" *US News & World Report*, February 12, 2007, 30–39.

p. 43, "Ethanol manufacturers want to . . .": Environmental Protection Agency, "Notice of Receipt of a Clean Air Act Waiver Application to Increase the Allowable Ethanol Content of Gasoline to 15 Percent; Request for Comment," April 15, 2009, www.epa.gov/ otaq/regs/fuels/additive/e15-increase.pdf (accessed April 16, 2009).

p. 43, "As of 2009 only about 2,000 of the . . .": United States Department of Energy, "Alternative Fueling Station Total Counts by State and Fuel Type," October 22, 2009, www.afdc.energy. gov/afdc/fuels/stations_counts.html?print (accessed October 28, 2009); Energy Information Administration, "Frequently Asked Questions—Gasoline," 2008, http://tonto.eia.doe.gov/ask/gasoline_ faqs.asp#retail_gasoline_stations (accessed October 28, 2009).

pp. 43–44, "The Congressional Budget Office found.. . .": Congression-al Budget Office, "The Impact of Ethanol Use on Food Prices and Greenhouse Gas Emissions," 6; Stephen Dinan, "Ethanol Policies Fuel Food-Price Rise," *Washington Times*, April 9, 2009, http://washingtontimes.com/news/2009/apr/09/ethanol-policies-fuel-food-price-rise/ (accessed April 9, 2009).

p. 44, "[T]he effect of transforming hundreds and . . .": Edith M. Lederer, "Production of Biofuels 'Is a Crime,'" the *Independent*, October 27, 2007, www.independent.co.uk/environment/green-living/production-of-biofuels-is-a-crime-398066.html (accessed May 5, 2009).

p. 44, "UN Food and Agriculture Organisation (FAO) . . .": IRIN, "UN Food Agency Regrets 'Crime Against Humanity' Label on Biofuels," November 1, 2007, www.alertnet.org/thenews/newsdesk/IRIN/bb8b991b20e2117c1b500c09ef639311.htm (accessed May 5, 2009).

pp. 44–45, "food and biofuels production . . .": John A. Matthews, "Opinion: Is Growing Biofuel Crops a Crime Against Humanity?" *Biofuels, Bioproducts, and Biorefining*, 2008, 97–99, www.gsm.mq.edu.au/wps/wcm/connect/174da2804bd3ee01aab5aebb537885fc/Growing+Biofuel+Crops.pdf?MOD=AJPERES&CACHEID=174da2804bd3ee01aab5aebb537885fc (accessed May 5, 2009).

p. 45, "Research by the Argonne National . . .": Michael Wang, May Wu, and Hong Huo, "Life-Cycle Energy and Greenhouse Gas Emission Impacts of Different Corn Ethanol Plant Types," *Environmental Research Letters*, May 22, 2007, www.iop.org/EJ/article/1748-9326/2/2/024001/erl7_2_024001.pdf?request-id=17e3aff4-ebc9-4c46-b97d-d26405f48e9e (accessed April 14, 2009).

p. 46, "By 2030 biofuels and other organic . . .": United States Department of Energy and United States Department of Agriculture, *Biomass as Feedstock for a Bioenergy and Bioproduct Industry: The Technical Feasibility of a Billion-ton Annual Supply*, Springfield, VA: National Technical Information Service, April 2005, i–ii, 3–4, 18–33, www1.eere.energy.gov/biomass/pdfs/final_billionton_vision_report2.pdf (accessed August 14, 2009).

p. 46, "by 2050, biofuel crops could take up as . . . .": Marine Biological Laboratory, "Thinking It Through: Scientists Call for Policy to Guide Biofuels Industry Toward Sustainable Practices," October 2, 2008, www.mbl.edu/news/press_releases/2008/2008_pr_10_02.html (accessed April 15, 2009); G. Philip Robertson et al., "Sustainable Biofuels Redux," *Science*, October 3, 2008, 49–50.

pp. 46–47, "Primate scientist Jane Goodall and . . .": Reuters, "Jane Goodall Says Biofuel Crops Hurt Rainforests," September 26, 2007, www.reuters.com/article/latestCrisis/idUSN26273329 (accessed April 15, 2009).

p. 47, "According to Holly Gibbs of Stanford . . .": Chelsea Anne Young, "Biofuels Boom Could Fuel Rainforest Destruction, Reports FSE Researcher Holly Gibbs," February 18, 2009, http://foodsecurity.stanford.edu/news/biofuels_boom_could_ fuel_rainforest_destruction_reports_fse_researcher_holly_ gibbs_20090218 (accessed February 5, 2010).

p. 47, "Researchers from Princeton University . . .": Timothy Searchinger, et al., "Use of U.S. Croplands for Biofuels Increases Greenhouse Gases Through Emissions from Land-Use Change," *Science*, February 29, 2008, 1238–1240; H. Josef Herbert, "Study: Ethanol May Add to Global Warming," *USA Today*, February 8, 2008, www.usatoday.com/weather/climate/globalwarming/2008- 02-08-ethanol-study_N.htm (accessed April 14, 2009).

p. 47, "The state of California considered corn ethanol's . . .": Jeff Tolefson, "California in Clean Fuel Drive," *Nature*, April 29, 2009, 1083, www.nature.com/news/2009/090429/full/4581083a.html (accessed April 29, 2009). pp. 48–49, "Biofuels generate income and employment . . .": Luiz Inácio Lula da Silva, "Address by the President of the Republic, Luiz Inácio Lula da Silva at the Opening of the Thirtieth Regional Conference for Latin America and the Caribbean," April 16, 2008, www.fao.org/newsroom/common/ ecg/1000831/en/Lula-speech.doc (accessed May 5, 2009).

p. 49, "We know sugarcane ethanol has the lowest . . .": UNICA, "Sugarcane Ethanol Industry Eager to Implement Renewable Fuel Standard," May 5, 2009, http://english.unica.com.br/releases/show. asp?rlsCode={4D7FEE18-11C4-412E-9E26-5F4B7831F4B3} (accessed May 5, 2009).

p. 50, "A 2009 study from the Paris-based . . .": "First Internation- al Science-Based Consensus on Biofuels' Environmental Impact," Cornell University press release, April 2, 2009, www.eeb.cornell.edu/ howarth/SCOPE%20Biofuels%20Press%20Release.pdf (accessed April 15, 2009); "Biofools," *Economist*, April 11, 2009, 81.

p. 50, "That finding is consistent with an . . .": P. J. Crutzen, et al., "N$_2$O Release from Agro-biofuel Production Negates Global Warming Reduction by Replacing Fossil Fuels," *Atmospheric Chemistry and Physics Discussions*, August 1, 2007, 11191–11205, www.atmos-chem-phys-discuss.net/7/11191/2007/acpd-7-11191-2007.pdf (accessed April 15, 2009).

p. 50, "The policy of using ethanol to reduce reliance . . .": R.W. Howarth and S. Bringezu, eds., "Biofuels: Environmental Consequences and Interactions with Changing Land Use," 2009, http://cip.cornell.edu/biofuels/ (accessed April 15, 2009).

p. 50, "Nelson's BioWillie fuel blends. . .":Greg Pahl, "Biodiesel: Homegrown Oil," *Mother Earth News*, February/March 2006, 65–71.

p. 52, "According to chemical engineer Joseph Schuster . . .": Joseph M. Shuster, *Beyond Fossil Fools: The Roadmap to Energy Independence by 2040*, Edina, MN: Beaver's Pond Press, 2008, 168.

p. 52, "Indeed, 1 acre of sunflowers . . .": Pahl, "Biodiesel: Homegrown Oil," *supra*.

p. 53, "About 60 percent of biomass electricity . . .": Paul Davidson, "Biomass Plants Find Power in Poop," *USA Today*, February 9, 2007, 4.

p. 53, "Already the United States has more . . .": Mark Jenner, "Biomass Energy Outlook," *BioCycle*, March 2009, 4.

Chapter 4

p. 55, "In his 2003 State of the Union address, President George W. Bush . . .": "Bush Touts Benefits of Hydrogen Economy," CNN, February 6, 2003, www.cnn.com/2003/ALLPOLITICS/02/06/bush-energy/index.html (accessed September 2, 2009); George W. Bush, "State of the Union Address," January 28, 2003, www.vlib.us/amdocs/texts/bush012003.html (accessed April 7, 2009).

p. 57, "The proton-exchange membranes, or PEMs . . ." David Strahan, "Whatever Happened to the Hydrogen Economy?" *New Scientist*, November 29, 2008, 40–43.

p. 57, "When Honda's FCX clarity . . .": Joseph Romm, "The Last Car You Would Ever Buy—Literally," *Technology Review*, June 18, 2008, www.technologyreview.com/blog/guest/22087/ (accessed April 8, 2009); Martin Fackler, "Latest Honda Runs on Hydrogen, Not Petroleum," *New York Times* Online, June 17, 2008, www.nytimes.com/2008/06/17/business/worldbusiness/17fuelcell.html?_r=3&adxnnl=1&oref=slogin&ref=worldbusiness&adxnnlx=1213733114-00vfwWQ+IeqQLLp5LQ9c9w (accessed April 8, 2009).

p. 58, "Researchers at the Massachusetts Institute . . .": Nancy Stauffer, "Hydrogen Vehicle Won't Be Viable Soon, Study Says," MIT News Office, March 5, 2003, http://web.mit.edu/newsoffice/2003/hydrogen-0305.html (accessed April 8, 2009).

p. 59, "The California Fuel Cell Partnership has . . .": Liane Yvkoff, "California to Get 46 Retail Hydrogen Stations by 2014," March 25, 2009, http://reviews.cnet.com/8301-13746_7-10204075-48.html (accessed April 8, 2009).

p. 59, "One concept comes from a British company . . .": David Strahan, "Whatever Happened to the Hydrogen Economy?" *New Scientist*, November 29, 2008, 40–43; ITM Power, www.itm-power.com/ (accessed April 8, 2009).

pp. 59–61, "Another process, proposed by Jerry . . .": "New Process Generates Hydrogen from Aluminum to Run Engines, Fuel Cells," Purdue University press release, May 15, 2007, http://news.uns.purdue.edu/x/2007a/070515WoodallHydrogen.html (accessed April 8, 2009).

p. 61, "Critics of hydrogen energy, such as Joseph . . .": Joseph Romm, "The Last Car You Would Ever Buy—Literally," *Technology Review*, June 18, 2008, www.technologyreview.com/blog/guest/22087/ (accessed April 8, 2009).

p. 62, "It is possible with the technology . . .": Maria Maack, e-mail to Kathiann M. Kowalski, April 9, 2009; Icelandic New Energy, www.newenergy.is/newenergy/en/, 2009 (accessed April 9, 2009).

p. 62, "By 2003 Shell had the world's first retail hydrogen fuel pump . . .": Colin Woodard, "Iceland Heads Toward Hydrogen Economy," *Christian Science Monitor*, February 11, 2009, 13–16; James Crugnale, "The Ghost Hydrogen Station," *Reykjavik Grapevine*, September 26, 2008, www.grapevine.is/Features/ReadArticle/ The-Ghost-Hydrogen-Station (accessed April 9, 2009).

p. 63, "The virtues of clean technology cost, but polluting does not cost . . .": Maria Maack, e-mail to Kathiann M. Kowalski, April 9, 2009.

Chapter 5

p. 65, "As a zero-carbon energy source, nuclear . . .": Department of Energy, "Secretary Chu Announces Funding for 71 University-Led Nuclear Research and Development Projects," May 6, 2009, www.ne.doe.gov/newsroom/2009PRs/nePR050609.html (accessed September 2, 2009); Amanda Leigh Mascarelli, "Funding Cut for US Nuclear Waste Dump," *Nature*, April 30, 2009, 1086–1087.

p. 65, "As of 2009 the industry's 104 reactors . . .": Nuclear Energy Institute, "Reliable & Affordable Energy," 2009, www.nei.org/ keyissues/reliableandaffordableenergy/ (accessed May 18, 2009).

p. 66, "Fission of a single gram of uranium can . . .": Walter Scheider, *A Serious But Not Ponderous Book About Nuclear Energy*, Ann Arbor, MI: Cavendish Press, 2001, 76.

p. 66, "Nuclear fission produces about a million times more energy. . .": Tony Rothman, e-mail to Kathiann M. Kowalski, June 25, 2009.

pp. 68–69, "Fears about nuclear power . . .": Donald Janson, "Radiation Is Released in Accident at Nuclear Plant in Pennsylvania," March 29, 1979, A1; *Washington Post*, "A Pump Failure and Claxon Alert," WashingtonPost.com, 1979, 1999 (accessed May 14, 2009); Walter Scheider, *A Serious But Not Ponderous Book About Nuclear Energy*, Ann Arbor, MI: Cavendish Press, 2001, 216–241.

p. 70, "Worries about sabotage surfaced when . . .": H. Josef Herbet, "'Embarrassing' Mistake Puts US Nuke List Online," *Washington Post* Online, June 3, 2009, www.washingtonpost.com/wp-dyn/content/article/2009/06/03/AR2009060300893.html (accessed June 4, 2009).

p. 73, "As this century opened . . .": Ingrid Kelley, *Energy in America: A Tour of Our Fossil Fuel Culture and Beyond,* Burlington: University of Vermont Press, 2008, 65.

p. 74, "Energy secretary Steven Chu told a Senate committee. . .": "John McCain and Steven Chu on Yucca Mountain," March 6, 2009, http://neinuclearnotes.blogspot.com/2009/03/john-mccain-and-steven-chu-on-yucca.html (accessed October 28, 2009); Amanda Leigh Mascarelli, "Funding Cut for US Nuclear Waste Dump," *Nature,* April 30, 2009, 1086–1087.

p. 74, "They only come in one size: extra large . . .": Al Gore, Testimony before Senate Committee on Foreign Relations, January 28, 2009, www.youtube.com/watch?v=IoYi2DGxABs&feature=PlayList&p=AA1657A7C7F28443&index=8 (accessed May 6, 2009).

p. 75, "The Nuclear Energy Institute maintains that . . .": Nuclear Energy Institute, "Electricity Supply," 2009, www.nei.org/keyissues/reliableandaffordableenergy/electricitysupply/ (accessed May 18, 2009).

p. 75, "Taking all costs into account, elecricity . . .": William Sweet, *Kicking the Carbon Habit: Global Warming and the Case for Renewable and Nuclear Energy,* New York: Columbia University Press, 2006, 187.

p. 76, "Nuclear energy advocates also . . .": Nuclear Energy Institute, "Electricity Supply," 2009, www.nei.org/keyissues/reliableandaffordableenergy/electricitysupply/ (accessed May 18, 2009).

p. 76, "Now the International Thermonuclear Experimental . . .": Charles Seife, "Free Energy: $15 Billion," *Discover,* October 2008, 32.

p. 76, "India aims to generate . . .": Amit Garg, "Strong Energy Sector Can Fuel Economy," *Daily News & Analysis*, India, April 22, 2009, www.dnaindia.com/report.asp?newsid=1249679 (accessed May 12, 2009).

p. 77, "We will be meeting 20 to 25 percent . . .": Promit Mukherjee, "'We Will Raise Capacity 5-fold in Five Years,'" *Daily News & Analysis*, India, October 13, 2008, www.npcil.nic.in/pdf/CMD_ PressStatement.pdf (accessed September 2, 2009).

p. 78, "Navy researcher Pamela Mosier-Boss reported on her group's work . . .": Mark T. Sampson, "Cold Fusion' Rebirth? New Evidence for Existence of Controversial Energy Source," American Chemical Society press release, March 23, 2009, http://portal.acs.org/portal/acs/corg/content?_nfpb=true&_ pageLabel=PP_ARTICLEMAIN&node_id=222&content_ id=WPCP_012362&use_sec=true&sec_url_var=region1&__ uuid=4cde3567-3e9e-437a-8f5f-8deee2799d2c (accessed June 5, 2009).

p. 79, "Others remain skeptical about . . .": David R. Butcher, "Scientists Claim Cold Fusion Breakthrough," April 14, 2009, http://news.thomasnet.com/IMT/archives/2009/04/scientists-claim-visual-evidence-of-cold-fusion-breakthrough.html (accessed May 11, 2009); AFP, "Cold Fusion 'Evidence' Unveiled," *Discovery News*, March 24, 2009, http://dsc.discovery.com/news/2009/03/24/cold-fusion.html (accessed May 11, 2009).

Chapter 6

p. 80, "Representatives of the . . .": "The U.S. Photovoltaic Industry Roadmap," 2003, www.nrel.gov/docs/gen/fy03/30150.pdf (accessed May 7, 2009).

p. 80, "In 2009 solar energy produced less . . .": *New York Times*, "Solar Energy," 2009, http://topics.nytimes.com/top/news/business/energy-environment/solar-energy/index.html (accessed May 8, 2009).

p. 83, "A report from the Palo Alto Research Center . . .": Palo Alto Research Center, "Technology Advances in Delivering Cost-Competitive Solar Energy," 2006, www.parc.com/content/attachments/Whitepaper-SolarEnergyTech.pdf (accessed June 5, 2009).

p. 87, "Of course, the sun does not strike . . .": Sandra Upson, "How Free Is Solar Energy?" *IEEE Spectrum*, February 2008, 72, www.spectrum.ieee.org/feb08/5930 (accessed May 8, 2009).

p. 87, "[I]f we took an area of the Southwestern . . .": Al Gore, Testimony before and Responses to Questions by Senate Foreign Relations Committee, January 28, 2009, www.politifact.com/truth-o-meter/statements/2009/feb/18/al-gore/al-gore-optimistic-about-solar-energy-and-pretty-a/ (accessed May 6, 2009); YouTube, "Al Gore (4 of 15) Senate Testimony," January 28, 2009, www.youtube.com/watch?v=DB-3-5Rj2m8&feature=PlayList&p=AA1657A7C7F28443&index=3 (accessed May 6, 2009).

p. 87, "Information from the Department of . . .": U.S. Department of Energy, "Learning About PV: The Myths of Solar Electricity," 2008, http://www1.eere.energy.gov/solar/myths.html (accessed May 6, 2009).

p. 88, "This technology has the potential . . .": University of Delaware, "UD-led Team Sets Solar Cell Record, Joins DuPont on $100 Million Project," July 23, 2007, www.udel.edu/PR/UDaily/2008/jul/solar072307.html (accessed May 8, 2009); "An Unexpected Discovery Could Yield a Full Spectrum Solar Cell," November 18, 2002, www.udel.edu/PR/UDaily/2008/jul/solar072307.html (accessed August 25, 2009); International Energy Agency, "Photovoltaic Cells," www.iea-pvps.org/pv/materials.htm (accessed August 25, 2009).

p. 88, "Another idea for dealing with the . . .": Cool Earth, "Breakthrough Solar Technology that Addresses the Global Energy Crisis," www.coolearthsolar.com/ (accessed May 8, 2009); Cool Earth Solar, "Our Breakthrough Technology (The Short Version)," www.coolearthsolar.com/technology (accessed May 8, 2009); Fred

Hapgood, "Rob Lamkin: Sunshine Superman," *Discover*, October 2008, 33; Martin LaMonica, "Cool Earth Solar Generates Power with 'Solar Balloons,'" February 14, 2008, www.coolearthsolar.com/technology (accessed May 8, 2009).

p. 88, "According to the Department of Energy . . .": U.S. Department of Energy, "Why PV Is Important to the Economy," 2008, http://www1.eere.energy.gov/solar/to_economy.html (accessed June 5, 2009).

p. 89, "Japan continues to be a major . . .": "Action Plan for Achieving a Low-carbon Society," July 29, 2008, 13, www.kantei.go.jp/foreign/policy/ondanka/final080729.pdf (accessed May 8, 2009); David Cyranoski, "Japan Goes for the Sun," *Nature*, April 30, 2009, 1084–1085; Japan for Sustainability, "Japanese Government Adopts Action Plan Emphasizing Solar Power Generation," January 1, 2009, www.japanfs.org/en/pages/028625.html (accessed May 8, 2009).

p. 90, "By 2008, the Department of Energy . . .": Department of Energy, "Learning about PV: The Myths of Solar Electricity," 2008, http://www1.eere.energy.gov/solar/myths.html (accessed May 7, 2009).

p. 90, "As of 2009, all but fourteen states . . .": Pew Center on Global Climate Change, "Renewable & Alternative Energy Portfolio Standards," December 14, 2009, www.pewclimate.org/what_s_being _done/in_the_states/rps.cfm (accessed February 16, 2010).

Chapter 7

p. 93, "According to a 2008 report from . . .": United States Department of Energy, "20% Wind Energy by 2030: Increasing Wind Energy's Contribution to U.S. Electricity Supply," July 2008, http://www1.eere.energy.gov/windandhydro/pdfs/41869.pdf (accessed January 20, 2008).

p. 93, "Since 1982, APWRA's 5,400 windmills . . .": Center for Biological Diversity, "Fact Sheet on Altamont Pass Bird Kills," www.biologicaldiversity.org/campaigns/protecting_birds_of_

prey_at_altamont_pass/pdfs/factsheet.pdf (accessed January 15, 2009).

p. 93, "Altamont Pass has become a death zone . . .": Center for Biological Diversity, "Lawsuit Seeks Redress for Massive Illegal Bird Kills at Altamont Pass, CA, Wind Farms," January 12, 2004, www.biologicaldiversity.org/news/press_releases/birdkills1-12-04. htm (accessed January 15, 2009).

pp. 93–94, "Jeff Miller at CBD argued that the . . . .": Hilary Watts, "Blades, Birds, and Bats: Wind Energy and Wildlife Not a Cut-and-Dried Issue," *High Country News*, May 2, 2005, www. hcn.org/issues/297/15484 (accessed January 15, 2009).

p. 94, "a 2008 study at the University of Calgary . . .": University of Calgary, "Bat Deaths from Wind Turbines Explained," August 25, 2008, www.ucalgary.ca/news/aug2008/batdeaths (accessed January 15, 2009).

p. 94, "I'm thrilled that this critical . . .": Bats and Wind Energy Cooperative, "Researchers Seek to Reduce Bat Deaths at Wind Turbines," October 14, 2008, www.batsandwind.org/pdf/BWEC%20 Curtailment%20Press%20Release10-14.pdf (accessed January 15, 2009);

pp. 94–95, "American Wind Energy Association [AWEA] says . . .": American Wind Energy Association, "AWEA Urges Academy to Conduct Study of All Energy Sources," May 3, 2007, www. awea.org/newsroom/releases/AWEA_Statement_on_NAS_ Study_05032007.html (accessed January 15, 2009).

p. 95, "On balance, Audubon strongly supports . . .": Audubon Society, "Congressional Testimony on Benefits of Wind Power," May 1, 2007, www.audubon.org/campaign/testimony_0507.html (accessed January 15, 2009).

p. 96, "some Cape Cod residents were staunchly . . .": Wendy Williams and Robert Whitcomb, *Cape Wind: Money, Celebrity, Class, Politics, and the Battle for Our Energy Future on Nantucket Sound*, New York: Public Affairs, 2007, 127–129.

p. 96, "As an environmentalist, I support wind power . . .": Robert F. Kennedy, Jr., "An Ill Wind Off Cape Cod," *New York Times,* December 16, 2005, www.nytimes.com/2005/12/16/opinion/ 16kennedy.html?_r=1 (accessed January 13, 2009).

p. 96, "This is visual pollution . . .": Williams and Whitcomb, *Cape Wind,* xii, xvi, 32, 90–97.

p. 96, "Nantucket Sound: Once It's Gone. . .": "Save Our Sound— Alliance to Protect Nantucket Sound," 2007, www.saveoursound. org/site/PageServer (accessed January 13, 2009).

p. 96, "It's really hypocritical . . .": "Jason Jones 180—Nantucket," *The Daily Show,* August 7, 2007, www.thedailyshow.com/video/ index.jhtml?videoId=91140&title=jason-jones-180-nantucket (accessed January 13, 2009).

p. 96, "Greenpeace USA supports the Cape . . .": Greenpeace, "Cape Wind Ad," 2007, www.greenpeace.org/usa/campaigns/ global-warming-and-energy/green-solutions/wind-power/cape-wind/cape-wind-ad (accessed January 13, 2009); Greenpeace USA, "Greenpeace Airs Ads to Reinforce Cape Wind Support," August 20, 2007, www.greenpeace.org/usa/press-center/releases2/ greenpeace-airs-ads-to-reinfor (accessed January 13, 2009).

pp. 96–97, "Given that all of the . . .": United States Senate Committee on Energy & Natural Resources, "Press Release: Cape Wind," December 18, 2008, http://energy.senate.gov/public/index. cfm?FuseAction=PressReleases.Detail&PressRelease_id=556f8dc3-4f55-4209-8692-e335670dd11c&Month=12&Year=2008&Part y=0 (accessed January 13, 2009); "Cape Wind Lauds Congressman Markey," November 9, 2009, http://www.capewind.org/news1024. htm (accessed February 5, 2010).

p. 97, "Wind energy is never going to be . . .": "Wind Jammers," *Wall Street Journal,* August 28, 2007, A12.

pp. 97–98, "In order to meet 20 percent of the . . .": United States Department of Energy, "20% Wind Energy by 2030: Increasing Wind Energy's Contribution to U.S. Electricity Supply," July 2008,

14, http://www1.eere.energy.gov/windandhydro/pdfs/41869.pdf (accessed February 5, 2010).

p. 98, "Presently, for every 100 miles . . .": Joseph M. Shuster, *Beyond Fossil Fools: The Roadmap to Energy Independence by 2040*, Edina, MN: Beaver's Pond Press, 2008, 149.

p. 99, "By 2007 wind power was meeting 19.7 . . .": Danish Energy Alliance, "Energy Statistics 2007," October 2008, 9, www.ens. dk/graphics/UK_Facts_Figures/Statistics/yearly_statistics/2007/ energy%20statistics%202007%20uk.pdf (accessed January 20, 2009); Danish Wind Energy Association, "Annual Report 2008," 4, www.windpower.org/media(2455,1033)/annual_report_2008. pdf (accessed May 18, 2009).

p. 99, "Danish companies have also captured . . .": Jay Yarrow, "GE Gaining Market Share in Wind Turbine Business (GE)," March 25, 2009, www.businessinsider.com/ge-gaining-market-share-in-wind-turbine-business-2009-3 (accessed October 28, 2009).

p. 99, "To bolster that support, the Danish . . .": Danish Wind Energy Association, www.windpower.org/en/core.htm and www. windpower.org/en/core.htm (accessed May 18, 2009).

p. 99, "Danish companies have also . . .": Ministry of Foreign Affairs of Denmark, "Danish Based Wind Turbine Companies Are Gaining Global Market Share," March 27, 2007, www.investindk. com/visNyhed.asp?artikelID=17181 (accessed January 20, 2009).

p. 99, "Within Europe, the UK is a . . .": Angelika Pullen, Global Wind Energy Association, e-mail to Kathiann M. Kowalski, May 11, 2009.

p. 101, "According to the Energy Information Administration, the United . . .": Energy Information Administration, "Energy Kid's Page: Geothermal Energy," July 2008, www.eia.doe.gov/kids/energyfacts/ sources/renewable/geothermal.html#Uses.(accessed May 19, 2009).

p. 101, "Geothermal power projects continue to . . .": Geothermal Energy Association, "Geothermal Power Continues Strong

Growth, New Industry Report Shows," March 4, 2009, http://geo-energy.org//publications/pressReleases/Geothermal_Power_Continues_Dramatic_Growth_Release%20_2_.pdf (accessed May 19, 2009).

pp. 101–102, "Nevertheless, a 2006 report from the . . .": Jefferson W. Tester et al., *The Future of Geothermal Energy*, Cambridge, MA: Massachusetts Institute of Technology, 2006, 1–9, 1–33, http://geothermal.inel.gov/publications/future_of_geothermal_energy.pdf (accessed May 19, 2009).

p. 102, "More than 70 percent of the country's . . .": Energy Information Administration, "Net Generation by Energy Source by Type of Producer, 1996 through 2007," January 21, 2009, www.eia.doe.gov/cneaf/electricity/epa/epaxlfile1_1.pdf (accessed May 20, 2009); Energy Information Administration, "Idaho," 2009, http://tonto.eia.doe.gov/state/state_energy_profiles.cfm?sid=ID (accessed May 20, 2009); Energy Information Administration, "Hydropower—Energy from Moving Water," October 2008, www.eia.doe.gov/kids/energyfacts/sources/renewable/water.html (accessed August 25, 2009).

p. 105, "This plant produces on average . . .": Robert Duran, e-mail to Kathiann M. Kowalski, August 26, 2009.

p. 106, "Various other devices can work . . .": Alok Jha, "Anaconda Wave-Power Generator Snakes into Next Stage of Production," May 6, 2009, www.guardian.co.uk/environment/2009/may/06/anaconda-wave-power (accessed August 25, 2009; Sonal Patel, "A New Wave: Ocean Power," *Power*, May 2008, 48–51, www.powermag.com/renewables/hydro/A-new-wave-Ocean-power_176.html (accessed June 5, 2009); U.S. Department of Energy, "Ocean Wave Energy," December 30, 2008, www.energysavers.gov/renewable_energy/ocean/index.cfm/mytopic=50009 (accessed May 21, 2009).

p. 106, "It took us more than four years . . .": David C. Holzman, "Blue Power: Turning Tides into Electricity," *Environmental Health Perspectives*, December 2007, A590–A593.

Chapter 8

pp. 107, 109, "More than 4 million flex-fuel . . .": Daniel J. Weiss and Nat Gryll, "Flex-Fuel Bait and Switch," June 18, 2007, www.americanprogress.org/issues/2007/06/flexfuel.html (accessed June 5, 2009).

p. 109, "when the federal government added . . .": Kimberly Kindy and Dan Keating, "Problems Plague U.S. Flex-Fuel Fleet: Most Government-Bought Vehicles Still Use Standard Gas," *Washington Post*, November 23, 2008, A1.

p. 109, "The electric-vehicle market failed to materialize . . .": Katharine Mieszkowski, "Steal This Car!" *Salon.com*, September 4, 2002, http://dir.salon.com/story/tech/feature/2002/09/04/woe_to_ev1/index.html (accessed June 2, 2009).

p. 109, "They're the cleanest cars ever made . . .": Mieszkowski, "Steal This Car!" September 4, 2002.

p. 110, "The expected price tag for General . . .": Alex Taylor III, "The Great Electric Car Race," *Fortune*, April 27, 2009, 38.

p. 110, "Gas prices would have to go to $8 a . . .": Taylor, "The Great Electric Car Race," April 27, 2009.

p. 111, "On any given day, 500,000 . . .": "Public's Tolerance of Outages Said to Be Falling," *Restructuring Today*, October 18, 2004, www.epri-intelligrid.com/intelligrid/docs/Restructuring_Today_101804.pdf (accessed May 29, 2009).

p. 111, "It's technologically . . .": Mark Bello, telephone interview with Kathiann M. Kowalski, May 28, 2009; Massoud Amin and Phillip F. Schewe, "Preventing Blackouts," *Scientific American*, May 2007, p. 60.

pp. 111–112, "power interruptions cost the country . . .": Lawrence Berkeley National Laboratory, "Berkeley Lab Study Estimates $80 Billion Annual Cost of Power Interruptions," February 2, 2005, www.lbl.gov/Science-Articles/Archive/EETD-power-interruptions.html (accessed May 29, 2009); Kristina Hamachi-La-Commare and Joe Eto, "Understanding the Cost of Power Inter-ruptions to U.S. Electricity Consumers," September 2004, http://certs.lbl.gov/pdf/55718.pdf (accessed May 29, 2009).

p. 112, "Basically, the amount of power . . .": Jim Owen, telephone interview with Kathiann M. Kowalski, October 3, 2003.

p. 112, "As more and more of your . . .": Mark Bello, telephone interview with Kathiann M. Kowalski, May 29, 2009.

p. 112, "The distribution of renewable sources . . .": Mark Bello, telephone interview with Kathiann M. Kowalski, May 29, 2009.

p. 113, "It cost about $100 million for a . . .": Matthew L. Wald, "A Little Give and Take on Electricity," *New York Times*, April 30, 2009, F1.

p. 114, "The Smart Grid is an urgent national . . .": Department of Energy, "Locke, Chu Announce Significant Steps in Smart Grid Development," May 18, 2009, www.energy.gov/news2009/7408. htm (accessed May 28, 2009); Lynne Kiesling, "Electric Intelligence: Establishing a Smart Grid Requires Regulatory Reform, Not Subsidies," *Reason*, June 2009, 26.

p. 114, "A compact fluorescent light bulb . . .": U.S. Environmental Protection Agency and U.S. Department of Energy, "Energy Star: Compact Fluorescent Bulbs for Consumers," www.energystar.gov/index.cfm?c=cfls.pr_cfls (accessed June 1, 2009).

Further Information

Books

Bishop, Amanda. *Energy Conservation.* New York: Marshall Cavendish Benchmark Books, 2009.

Casper, Julie Kerr. *Energy: Powering the Past, Present, and Future.* New York: Chelsea House Publishers, 2007.

Currie-McGhee, Leanne. *Biofuels.* San Diego: ReferencePoint Press, 2010.

Fridell, Ron. *Earth-Friendly Energy.* Minneapolis, MN: Lerner Publications, 2009.

Friedman, Lauri S., ed. *Energy Alternatives.* Farmington, MI: Greenhaven Press, 2006.

Giacobello, John. *Nuclear Power of the Future.* New York: Rosen Publishing Group, 2003.

Jones, Susan. *Solar Power of the Future.* New York: Rosen Publishing Group, 2003.

Langwith, Jacqueline, ed. *Renewable Energy.* Detroit: Greenhaven Press, 2009.

Mason, Paul. *How Big Is Your Energy Footprint?* New York: Marshall Cavendish Benchmark Books, 2009.

McCaffrey, Paul, ed. *U.S. National Debate Topic, 2008–2009: Alternative Energy.* New York: H. W. Wilson Co., 2008.

McNamee, Gregory. *Careers in Renewable Energy.* Masonville, CO: PixyJack Press, 2008.

Morgan, Sally. *From Windmills to Hydrogen Fuel Cells: Discovering Alternative Energy.* Chicago: Heinemann Library, 2007.

Nakaya, Andrea C. *Energy Alternatives.* San Diego: ReferencePoint Press, 2008.

Parks, Peggy J. *Solar Power.* San Diego: ReferencePoint Press, 2010.

Povey, Karen D. *Energy Alternatives.* Detroit: Thomson Gale, 2007.

Richards, Julie. *Nuclear Energy.* New York: Marshall Cavendish Benchmark Books, 2009.

_____. *Wind Energy.* New York: Marshall Cavendish Benchmark Books, 2009.

Saunders, Nigel, and Steven Chapman. *Renewable Energy.* Chicago: Raintree, 2006.

Snedden, Robert. *Energy Alternatives.* Chicago: Heinemann Library, 2006.

Tabak, John. *Wind and Water.* New York: Facts on File, 2009.

Organizations and Websites

Alternative Energy News
www.alternative-energy-news.info

American Solar Energy Society
www.ases.org

American Wind Energy Association
www.awea.org

Department of Energy
www.energy.gov

Energy Information Administration
www.eia.doe.gov

Nuclear Energy Institute
www.nei.org

Pew Research Center
http://pewresearch.org/topics/energyandenvironment

Pickens Plan
www.pickensplan.com/index.php

Reality Coalition
www.thisisreality.org

Solar Energy Industries Association
www.seia.org

Stanford University Global Climate and Energy Project
http://gcep.stanford.edu

Union of Concerned Scientists
www.ucsusa.org

Bibliography

Aeschbach-Hertig, Werner. "Clean Coal and Sparkling Water." *Nature*, April 2, 2009, 583–584.

Ansolabehere, Stephen, et al. "The Future of Nuclear Technology." Massachusetts Institute of Technology, 2003, http://web.mit.edu/nuclearpower/pdf/nuclearpower-summary.pdf and http://web.mit.edu/nuclearpower/pdf/nuclearpower-ch4-9.pdf (accessed May 18, 2009).

Boyle, Godfrey, ed. *Renewable Energy*. New York: Oxford University Press, 2004.

Congressional Budget Office. "The Impact of Ethanol Use on Food Prices and Greenhouse Gas Emissions." April 2009, www.cbo.gov/ftpdocs/100xx/doc10057/04-08-Ethanol.pdf (accessed April 14, 2009).

Department of Energy. *The Smart Grid: An Introduction*. 2008, www.oe.energy.gov/DocumentsandMedia/DOE_SG_Book_Single_Pages(1).pdf (accessed May 27, 2009).

Dinan, Stephen. "Ethanol Policies Fuel Food-Price Rise." *Washington Times*, April 9, 2009, http://washingtontimes.com/news/2009/apr/09/ethanol-policies-fuel-food-price-rise/ (accessed April 9, 2009).

Electric Power Research Institute. "Assessment of Achievable Potential from Energy Efficiency and Demand Response Programs in the U.S. (2010–2030): Executive Summary." http://mydocs. epri.com/docs/public/000000000001018363.pdf (accessed April 9, 2009).

Gilfillan, Stuart M. V., et al. "Solubility Trapping in Formation Water as Dominant CO_2 Sink in Natural Gas Fields." *Nature*, April 2, 2009, 614–618.

Heiman, Michael K., and Barry D. Solomon. "Fueling U.S. Transportation: The Hydrogen Economy and Its Alternatives." *Environment*, October 2007, 10–25.

Holzman, David C. "Blue Power: Turning Tides into Electricity." *Environmental Health Perspectives*, December 2007, A590–A593.

Hutchinson, Alex. "The Next Atomic Age: Can Safe Nuclear Power Work for America?" *Popular Mechanics*, October 2006, 76, www. popularmechanics.com/science/research/3760347.html?page=3 (accessed April 8, 2009).

Intergovernmental Panel on Climate Change (IPCC). "Climate Change 2007—Synthesis Report: Summary for Policymakers." November 2007, www.ipcc.ch/pdf/assessment-report/ar4/syr/ar4_ syr_spm.pdf (accessed January 12, 2009).

International Energy Agency. *World Energy Outlook 2008.* Paris: IEA Publications, 2008, http://weo.iea.org/Book/WEO2008.pdf (accessed May 8, 2008).

Kelley, Ingrid. *Energy in America: A Tour of Our Fossil Fuel Culture and Beyond.* Burlington: University of Vermont Press, 2008.

Lavelle, Marianne, and Bret Schulte. "Is Ethanol the Answer?" *US News & World Report*, February 12, 2007, 30–39.

Liebrand, Carolyn, and K. Charles Ling. "Switching on Cow Power." *Rural Cooperatives*, January/February 2009, 18–21.

Lowenstein, Roger. "What Price Oil?" *New York Times Magazine*, October 19, 2008, 46, 48.

Mascarelli, Amanda Leigh. "Funding Cut for US Nuclear Waste Dump." *Nature*, April 30, 2009, 1086–1087.

Matthews, John A. "Opinion: Is Growing Biofuel Crops a Crime Against Humanity?" *Biofuels, Bioproducts, and Biorefining*, 2008, 97–99, www.gsm.mq.edu.au/wps/wcm/connect/174da2804bd3ee 01aab5aebb537885fc/Growing+Biofuel+Crops.pdf?MOD=AJPER ES&CACHEID=174da2804bd3ee01aab5aebb537885fc (accessed May 5, 2009).

McKinsey & Company. "Carbon Capture & Storage: Assessing the Economics." 2008, www.mckinsey.com/clientservice/ccsi/pdf/ CCS_Assessing_the_Economics.pdf (accessed February 25, 2009).

Motavalli, Jim. "Nuclear Hydrogen: The Clean Byproduct." *E Magazine*, July/August 2007, 33.

O'Carroll, Eoin. "What Is Clean Coal Anyway?" *Christian Science Monitor*, October 17, 2008, http://features.csmonitor.com/environ ment/2008/10/17/what-is-clean-coal-anyway/ (accessed February 25, 2009).

Organisation for Economic Co-operation and Development. *World Energy Outlook 2008*. Paris: International Energy Agency, 2008.

Pahl, Greg. "Biodiesel: Homegrown Oil." *Mother Earth News*, February/March 2006, 65–71.

Palo Alto Research Center. "Technology Advances in Delivering Cost-Competitive Solar Energy." 2006, www.parc.com/content/attachments/Whitepaper-SolarEnergyTech.pdf (accessed June 5, 2009).

Patel, Sonal. "A New Wave: Ocean Power." *Power*, May 2008, 48–51, www.powermag.com/renewables/hydro/A-new-wave-Ocean-power_176.html (accessed June 5, 2009).

Romm, Joseph. "The Last Car You Would Ever Buy—Literally." *Technology Review*, June 18, 2008, www.technologyreview.com/blog/guest/22087/ (accessed April 8, 2009).

Scheider, Walter. *A Serious But Not Ponderous Book About Nuclear Energy*. Ann Arbor, MI: Cavendish Press, 2001.

Searchinger, Timothy, et al. "Use of U.S. Croplands for Biofuels Increases Greenhouse Gases Through Emissions from Land-Use Change." *Science*, February 29, 2008, 1238–1240.

Shuster, Joseph M. *Beyond Fossil Fools: The Roadmap to Energy Independence by 2040*. Edina, MN: Beaver's Pond Press, 2008.

Siegel, Jeff, with Chris Nelder and Nick Hodge. *Investing in Renewable Energy: Making Money on Green Chip Stocks*. Hoboken, NJ: John Wiley & Sons, 2008.

Strahan, David. "Whatever Happened to the Hydrogen Economy?" *New Scientist*, November 29, 2008, 40–43.

Sweet, William. *Kicking the Carbon Habit: Global Warming and the Case for Renewable and Nuclear Energy.* New York: Columbia University Press, 2006.

Tester, Jefferson W., et al. *The Future of Geothermal Energy.* Cambridge, MA: Massachusetts Institute of Technology, 2006. http://geothermal.inel.gov/publications/future_of_geothermal_energy.pdf (accessed May 19, 2009).

Wald, Matthew. "Questions About a Hydrogen Economy." *Scientific American,* May 2004, 66–73.

Wang, Michael, May Wu, and Hong Huo. "Life-Cycle Energy and Greenhouse Gas Emission Impacts of Different Corn Ethanol Plant Types." *Environmental Research Letters,* May 22, 2007, www.iop.org/EJ/article/1748-9326/2/2/024001/erl7_2_024001.pdf?request-id=17e3aff4-ebc9-4c46-b97d-d26405f48e9e (accessed April 14, 2009).

Williams, Wendy, and Robert Whitcomb. *Cape Wind: Money, Celebrity, Class, Politics, and the Battle for Our Energy Future on Nantucket Sound.* New York: Public Affairs, 2007.

Woodard, Colin. "Iceland Heads Toward Hydrogen Economy." *Christian Science Monitor,* February 11, 2009, 13–16.

Index

Page numbers in **boldface** are illustrations, tables, and charts.

About the Author

KATHIANN M. KOWALSKI has written twenty-two books and more than 540 articles and stories for young people. Kowalski received her bachelor's degree in political science from Hofstra University. She obtained her law degree from Harvard Law School, where she was an editor of the *Harvard Law Review*, and has practiced in the areas of litigation, corporate counseling, and environmental law. Kowalski's books have won awards from the Society of School Librarians International, the American Society for the Prevention of Cruelty to Animals, the Pennsylvania School Librarians Association, the National Science Teachers Association and the Children's Book Council. Kowalski was also awarded a Science Journalism Fellowship at the Marine Biological Laboratory. Her most recent book for Marshall Cavendish Benchmark was *National Health Care* in the Open for Debate series.